The Leader's Guide to Coaching in Schools

For Vicki
Generous, patient, unfailing supporter on the journey

—John

For Cathia
Relentlessly supportive and loving

—Christian

The Leader's Guide to Coaching in Schools

Creating Conditions for Effective Learning

John Campbell

Christian van Nieuwerburgh

Foreword by Jim Knight

A JOINT PUBLICATION

A SAGE Publishing Company

THE PROFESSIONAL LEARNING ASSOCIATION

FOR INFORMATION:

Corwin

A SAGE Company

2455 Teller Road

Thousand Oaks, California 91320

(800) 233-9936

www.corwin.com

SAGE Publications Ltd.

1 Oliver's Yard

55 City Road

London EC1Y 1SP

United Kingdom

SAGE Publications India Pvt. Ltd.

B 1/I 1 Mohan Cooperative Industrial Area

Mathura Road, New Delhi 110 044

India

SAGE Publications Asia-Pacific Pte. Ltd.

3 Church Street

#10-04 Samsung Hub

Singapore 049483

Program Director: Dan Alpert

Senior Associate Editor: Kimberly Greenberg

Associate Editor: Lucas Schleicher

Senior Editorial Assistant: Katie Crilley

Production Editor: Melanie Birdsall

Copy Editor: Deanna Noga

Typesetter: C&M Digitals (P) Ltd.

Proofreader: Laura Webb

Indexer: Mary Mortensen

Cover Designer: Candice Harman

Marketing Manager: Charline Maher

Printed in the United States of America

ISBN 978-1-5063-3583-4

This book is printed on acid-free paper.

SUSTAINABLE FORESTRY INITIATIVE
Certified Chain of Custody
Promoting Sustainable Forestry
www.sfiprogram.org
SFI-01268
SFI label applies to text stock

17 18 19 20 21 10 9 8 7 6 5 4 3 2

Contents

List of Videos

Watch It in Practice

Note From the Publisher: The authors have provided video and web content throughout the book that is available to you through QR (quick response) codes. To read a QR code, you must have a smartphone or tablet with a camera. We recommend that you download a QR code reader app that is made specifically for your phone or tablet brand.

Videos may also be accessed at
resources.corwin.com/campbellcoaching

Foreword

Although John Campbell lives in Sydney, Australia, and Christian van Nieuwerburgh lives in Leamington Spa, England, I've been fortunate to know them both for close to a decade. Fate, good luck, or something else has allowed us to work together on multiple occasions, and over that time, we have become good friends. Our friendship has grown in part because we share a deep commitment to finding ways to foster better lives for students and educators, and in part because we have taught and learned from each other through our collaboration, writing, and many, many conversations. Most important, I am grateful for their friendship because they are simply good people who lift my spirits and make me think whenever we get together.

Reading *The Leader's Guide to Coaching in Schools* has brought home to me all three of those aspects of our friendship. When you read this book, I'm quite confident that you will see, as I do, John and Christian's overall deep commitment to the well-being of students and educators. This book is written so that administrators, coaches, parents, students, and teachers can all use coaching strategies to, as John and Christian write, enhance the "learning and development" of others. Anyone who is interested in making a difference—and shouldn't that be all of us?—will find a lot here to help them have a positive impact on the lives of others.

One aspect of this book that I really appreciate is the authors' ability to give us a strong theoretical foundation for understanding coaching while describing those theories in a way that keeps the practical reality of coaching and learning front and center. As Kurt Lewin famously stated, "There is nothing as practical as a good theory." John and Christian bring that statement to life by writing in a clear and easy-to-understand way about theories such as solution-focused coaching, positive psychology, self-determination theory, and the importance of hope, and also by providing dozens of resources (questions to ask, books to read, coaching scaffolds to use, ideas to ponder) that any coach will find useful. The book, in other words, clearly explains many theories we need to know to get a deeper understanding of coaching, and it gives us numerous tools we can use to be better coaches.

The Leader's Guide to Coaching in Schools will also make you think about what it is you do, and push you to ask yourself some important questions.

Although people with strongly held beliefs about coaching may disagree with some of the ideas here, they shouldn't let that hold them back on the learning this book offers to anyone. When John, Christian, and I get together to talk, for example, we often disagree about how to define coaching. After twenty years studying instructional coaching, I have come to define instructional coaches as educators who "partner with teachers to analyze current reality, set goals, identify and explain teaching strategies to meet goals, and provide support until the goals are met" (Knight, 2017). While there are differences between my conceptualization of coaching and that of John and Christian's, I would encourage our readers to allow themselves to experience diverse perspectives.

At times, you too may question how this book explores what coaching is and how it should be done, and you may not agree with each opinion you read here; nevertheless, please don't let your differences keep you from learning. Anyone who is interested in coaching can learn from John Campbell and Christian van Nieuwerburgh, and this book is an excellent place to start. You will know more about coaching and be a better coach, no matter who you are, if you read *The Leader's Guide to Coaching in Schools*. I am certainly a more knowledgeable, better coach because of what I've read, and I'm grateful for all I've learned from the authors. In fact, I can't wait for our next conversation.

—Jim Knight
President, Instructional Coaching Group
and the Impact Research Lab
Research Associate, University of Kansas Center
for Research on Learning
Author, *The Impact Cycle, Better Conversations,*
and *Focus on Teaching*

REFERENCE

Knight, J. (2017). *The impact cycle: What good instructional coaches should do to foster powerful improvements in teaching.* Thousand Oaks, CA: Corwin.

Preface

This has been a wonderful project that we have both enjoyed immensely. It is a subject that is close to both our hearts. In one way or another, we have been interested in professional development, human growth, and education all our lives.

Having worked in the field of "coaching in education" for about a decade now, we are delighted to see the area continue to flourish. Since the publication of *Coaching in Education: Getting Better Results for Students, Educators and Parents* in 2012 highlighted the use of coaching in schools in the UK, the United States, and Australia, we have witnessed significant growth within the field. In some cases, we have been directly involved in supporting the application and implementation of coaching initiatives in schools and colleges in different parts of the world. Our Global Framework for Coaching in Education (2015) was our first attempt to capture and celebrate the breadth and quality of work taking place all over the world. We call the four quadrants of the Global Framework the *playing field* of coaching in education, and we're keen to encourage and enable the sharing of best practice internationally. We are lucky to have had the opportunities to work with educators in South America, the United States, Spain, Australia, New Zealand, the United Kingdom, and the Middle East. And what we're noticing is that there is continued enthusiasm from educators, learners, and leaders for coaching. We admire their work and hope that this book will support this enthusiasm and provide further encouragement to educators and leaders who want to support their learners and colleagues to be successful.

To capitalize on this international interest, we believe that it is important to bring some definitional clarity to the excellent work that is already taking place. Currently, the term *coaching* is being used to refer to a wide range of interventions in schools. In this book, we bring more consistency to the use of terminology, and we do this by delineating the boundaries between coaching and mentoring, defining the term *coaching in education*, and exploring the nuanced differences between formal coaching and a *coaching approach*. We are particularly encouraged by the potential for coaching conversations, both formal and informal, to make a contribution to almost any school improvement initiative.

For the sake of clarity and simplicity, we have used the pronouns *she* and *her* throughout. Unless we are referencing a particular person, please take *she* to denote "he or she" and *her* to denote "his or her." We hope that this makes the text easier to read.

As coauthors, we have enjoyed the process of working on this text together both personally and professionally. The process of writing has involved much reading, many conversations with colleagues, practitioners, and academics. We are committed to "research-informed practice," but primarily interested in the application of coaching in schools to make a difference, ultimately, to the experience of learners. The amount of research that is currently available is encouraging—and there is more work to do. We hope that this book builds on what we know already and raises new questions that need to be investigated further.

We sincerely hope that you find this book useful as you think about ways of enhancing the impact of coaching in your educational context.

Acknowledgments

We have been incredibly fortunate for the support that has been generously offered by colleagues, friends, and clients.

This book would not have been possible without the expert guidance and encouragement of Dan Alpert. He has been our mentor and strongest supporter. We are also grateful to colleagues at Corwin for making the process smooth and manageable, especially Katie Crilley, Melanie Birdsall, and Charline Maher.

We have been inspired by leading figures in the field of coaching, including Dr. Suzy Green of the Positivity Institute and Dr. Jim Knight of the Instructional Coaching Group, and recognize their valuable and pioneering contribution to the field of coaching in education. We wish to acknowledge the significant intellectual debt we owe to Dr. Tony Grant at the University of Sydney. His groundbreaking work in coaching has contributed greatly to the development of coaching psychology worldwide.

We are continually inspired by the work of our colleagues within Growth Coaching International (GCI). We are especially thankful to the late Mandy O'Bree, the founder of Growth Coaching International and the initial developer of the GROWTH model. We are grateful to Annette Gray, Kris Needham, Jason Pascoe, Grant O'Sullivan, and Chris Munro for reading and commenting on early drafts of this book. Margaret Barr, Kerry Mitchell, and Joellen Killion have generously shared their insights and experiences of coaching and the professional review of teachers. We are grateful to work with inspirational colleagues, including Andrea Giraldez, Andrea Berkeley, and Raja'a Allaho, who support GCI's international work, developing our programs in the Spanish-speaking world, the UK, and the Middle East.

We consider ourselves exceptionally fortunate to have the opportunity to work with such committed and passionate people. We wish to thank all the amazing educators with whom we have the opportunity to meet and collaborate. Ultimately, the purpose of this book is to support the wonderful work that you do.

PUBLISHER'S ACKNOWLEDGMENTS

Corwin gratefully acknowledges the contributions of the following reviewers:

Lydia Adegbola, Assistant Principal
Marta Valle High School
New York, NY

Elizabeth Alvarez, Principal
Chicago Public Schools
Chicago, IL

Sara Armstrong, Consultant and Past Educator
Berkeley, CA

Gary Bloom, Author and Retired Superintendent
Aptos, CA

R. Daniel Cunningham, Lecturer, Educational Leadership
    Program Coordinator
McDaniel College
Westminster, MD

Peter Dillon, Superintendent of Schools
Berkshire Hills Regional School District
Stockbridge, MA

Kelli Etheredge, Director of Teaching and Learning
St. Paul's Episcopal School
Mobile, AL

B. R. Jones, Superintendent of Education
Tate County School District
Senatobia, MS

Nicky Kemp, Assistant Superintendent
North Callaway R-1 School District
Kingdom City, MO

Diana Peer, Master Principal Leader
Arkansas Leadership Academy and University of Arkansas
Fayetteville, AR

William Sommers, Author
Austin, TX

About the Authors

John Campbell is Executive Director of Growth Coaching International Pty Ltd., an Australian-based consulting organization that provides coaching and coaching services to school leaders and teachers across Australia and in the UK, the Middle East, and the Asia/Pacific region.

John has been a high school teacher and a curriculum consultant and over the last decade has led leadership and coaching skill development workshops for thousands of educators across Australia and internationally.

In addition to his teaching degrees, he holds master's degrees in organizational communication and in the psychology of coaching from the University of Sydney.

Professor Christian van Nieuwerburgh is a well-respected executive coach, an internationally recognized academic, and a sought-after consultant. Christian is Professor of Coaching and Positive Psychology at the University of East London (UK). Regarded as an international authority in the field, he regularly speaks at conferences, facilitates training, and consults in the UK, Europe, Australia, and the Middle East.

Particularly passionate about the application of coaching and positive psychology in educational, organizational, and leadership contexts, he is the Editor-in-Chief of *Coaching: An International Journal of Theory, Research and Practice*. He is also the editor of two books that focus on this topic: *Coaching in Education: Getting Better Results for Students, Educators and Parents* (2012) and *Coaching in Professional Contexts* (2016). He is the author of *An Introduction to Coaching Skills: A Practical Guide* (2014, 2017). Through his role at Growth Coaching International, Christian continues to enjoy delivering training and professional development opportunities in schools, colleges, and universities.

CHAPTER 1

Coaching in Schools
An Introduction to the Global Framework for Coaching in Education

WELCOME!

Welcome to *The Leader's Guide to Coaching in Schools*! We are delighted that you are interested in the potential and possibilities of coaching within your educational context. This is a research-informed and evidence-based book that focuses on effective practice. Like you, we are interested in the *difference* that coaching can make to students, teachers and educational leaders. Our aim is to provide educational leaders with information and insights that can support them as they introduce or embed coaching practices and cultures within their educational institutions. The concepts and practical interventions presented in this book are based on latest research, theory and best practice. As coauthors, we both have in-depth practical experience of delivering coaching programs and training within educational institutions over many years. We both started our careers as teachers, and we are as passionate about the power of education today as we have ever been. We sincerely hope that this book will support you to maximize the potential of students and educators within your institution.

THE STRUCTURE OF THIS BOOK

There are 10 chapters:

1. Coaching in Schools: An Introduction to the Global Framework for Coaching in Education: This chapter presents an overview of the Global Framework for Coaching in Education to provide a broad conceptual framework and context for coaching in schools.

2. What Is Leadership Coaching? We provide some key definitions in this chapter to support our exploration of leadership coaching. The key differences between coaching and mentoring are presented. We also discuss the differences between coaching and using a coaching approach.

3. **The GROWTH Coaching System:** This chapter outlines a system that provides the basis for many coaching programs in educational institutions. The system includes a coaching framework, a set of conversational skills, and a particular way of being.

4. **Applying the Eight-Step Coaching Framework:** This chapter provides detailed information about the conversational process called the GROWTH framework.

5. **Positive, Strength-Based Approaches Underpinning the GCI Coaching System:** The solution-focused approach underpins the GROWTH Coaching System and is ideally suited for use in educational contexts. Positive, strength-based approaches are explored in this chapter.

6. **Using a Coaching Approach to Enhance the Performance and Well-Being of Teachers:** This chapter considers how a coaching approach can support performance review processes for educators.

7. **Creating the Right Context for Feedback:** The important role of giving and receiving feedback is explored in this chapter. It is considered in the context of leaders adopting a coaching approach.

8. **Using Coaching Approaches to Enhance the Performance and Well-Being of Teams:** Issues, techniques, and practices that leaders can use with their teams are presented in this chapter.

9. **Leading a Coaching Culture:** The concept of a *coaching culture* is discussed in this chapter. Strategic and practical ideas for encouraging a coaching culture are presented.

10. **Conclusion:** The final chapter reviews the main concepts covered in the book and looks to the future of coaching in schools.

COACHING IN EDUCATION

The good news is that the use of coaching in educational settings continues to flourish. Initially attracting interest in the late 20th century, coaching is now recognized globally as a powerful intervention that can support educators and learners (Campbell, 2016; Knight & van Nieuwerburgh, 2012; van Nieuwerburgh, 2012; van Nieuwerburgh & Barr, 2017). It has received support from many national, strategic educational organizations such as Learning Forward (https://learningforward.org/consulting/coaches-academy) in the United States, the Department for Education and Skills (2003), the National College for School Leadership (Creasy & Paterson, 2005), the Scottish College for Educational Leadership (2016) in the UK, and the Australian Institute for Teaching and School Leadership (2016) in Australia. Furthermore, there is a growing body of research (van Nieuwerburgh & Barr, 2016) that is providing an increasingly strong evidence base for its use in schools. And perhaps even more important, teachers and educational leaders in schools and colleges around the world are experiencing for themselves the transformative effect that coaching can have on themselves and others.

THE NATURAL HOME OF COACHING

While many assume that coaching has been imported into education from other fields such as sports or psychology, it is reasonable to argue that education is the natural home of coaching. In fact, the first recorded use of the term *coaching* to refer to a one-to-one supportive relationship occurred in an educational setting. Etymologically, the word *coach* was used to denote a type of horse-drawn carriage called a *kocsi*. It was called that in the Hungarian language because these carriages were built in a village called Kocs. In the 1830s, educators at the University of Oxford extended the concept of a vehicle that takes a person from Point A to Point B by using the term *coach* as slang to refer to a tutor who supports students to pass exams. In other words, the tutor (or coach) would take a person from "not knowing enough" (Point A) to "knowing enough to pass the exam" (Point B). Notably, the first recorded use of the word *coach* in an athletic sense did not occur until 1861, some three decades after its use in an educational setting. In any case, it seems logical to argue that places of learning (such as schools, colleges, and universities) are ideal places for coaching to flourish. Coaching and education share the same purpose: helping people learn, grow, and develop. Furthermore, some people would argue that coaching is simply a form of personalized learning. We believe that every coaching session is essentially a conversation about learning.

OUR DEFINITION OF COACHING IN EDUCATION

One of the challenges facing the profession of coaching is a lack of definitional clarity. There are many definitions of coaching, and people can understand the term differently. However, there is general agreement that coaching is "a managed conversation that takes place between two people," that it "aims to support sustainable change to behaviors or ways of thinking," and that it "focuses on learning and development" (van Nieuwerburgh, 2017, p. 5).

The phrase "coaching in education" is used to cover a range of interventions and approaches that are designed to improve the performance and well-being of learners and educators. For the purposes of this book, we are using the following definition:

> A one-to-one conversation that focuses on the enhancement of learning and development through increasing self-awareness and a sense of personal responsibility, where the coach facilitates the self-directed

learning of the coachee through questioning, active listening, and appropriate challenge in a supportive and encouraging climate. (van Nieuwerburgh, 2012, p. 17)

Educational leaders will immediately notice some important elements within this definition. First, educational leaders are ultimately responsible for enhancing "learning and development" opportunities within their institutions. They will also be interested in encouraging higher levels of "self-awareness," "personal responsibility," and "self-directed learning" in students and staff within the organization. Finally, educational leaders will appreciate the importance of creating "supportive and encouraging" educational environments. Coaching in education, therefore, can be a powerful way of empowering learners, increasing engagement, and creating positive learning cultures.

THE GLOBAL FRAMEWORK FOR COACHING IN EDUCATION

In response to the growing popularity of coaching in schools and colleges all over the world, the Global Framework for Coaching in Education has been devised (van Nieuwerburgh, Campbell, & Knight, 2015). Its purpose is to provide an inclusive playing field that incorporates the broadest range of coaching interventions. The playing field is divided into four quadrants, also called *portals* (see Figure 1.1). The portals represent ways in which coaching can be used effectively in educational settings. Each is a "way in" to introducing coaching within schools, colleges, or universities.

The framework can be a valuable tool for an educational leader. First, it can be used to assess the extent to which an organization is already using coaching within the different portals. Second, the framework provides four entry points for those seeking to introduce coaching into an institution. Third, the framework can offer ideas about the best coaching initiatives to use to have an impact where it is most needed. Fourth, it helps provide a focus for further research in the field of coaching in education. And finally, the framework allows leaders to take a strategic view of coaching within their organizations. The framework is a work-in-progress because the field is young and continually developing. There is no correct order of opening each of the portals. Each school or educational leader is best placed to decide where to start. Given the focus of this book, we begin by presenting the Educational Leadership portal.

EDUCATIONAL LEADERSHIP

As a leader yourself, you will be aware of the critically significant role that school, college, and university leaders play within their organizations. The educational leadership portal covers a range of interventions that can improve the quality of leadership in educational institutions and provide

FIGURE 1.1   The Global Framework for Coaching in Education

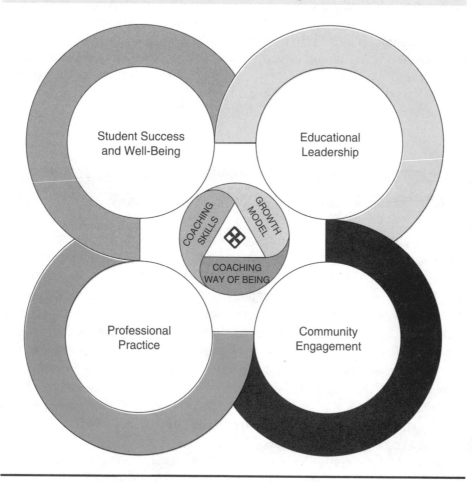

Student Success and Well-Being

Educational Leadership

COACHING SKILLS

GROWTH MODEL

COACHING WAY OF BEING

Professional Practice

Community Engagement

SOURCE: © Growth Coaching International.

personalized support to leaders. Broadly speaking, the two main areas of interest are giving educational leaders access to executive coaching and training principals to become coaches.

Leaders Having Access to Executive Coaching

It has often been suggested that being a principal can be a lonely job. With the level of responsibility vested in the role and the variable characteristics of the reporting line to a governing body or administrators, school leaders can find themselves feeling relatively unsupported at times. For these reasons, ensuring that leaders have access to an executive coach can be helpful. One qualitative study suggested that principals found access to a coach helpful for their leadership practice (James-Ward, 2013). In many authorities and districts, first-time principals are automatically provided with mentors.

This is excellent practice because some advice and support will be needed as the new leadership role is embraced. We propose, however, that newly appointed principals (who are experienced leaders and taking up positions in new schools) might find more value in having access to a coach. This is because the leaders would already bring considerable experience and skills to the role and could benefit from a thinking partner to consider the positive impact that they would like to have on their new institutions. In this regard, programs such as "first 100 days" might be helpful (see box).

IN CONTEXT: First 100 Days Coaching

This type of coaching program is designed to support principals during their first 100 days in a new school. It is a powerful way of providing additional strategic support during a very important period in a leader's professional life. Often, the tone of a leader's style and her vision is set during this initial period. Ideally, the school leader would have access to the coach as soon as she has been appointed. During the contracting phase, it would be made clear that the coaching agreement would conclude 100 days into the new principal's contract at the school. This helps focus minds and ensures that no sense of dependency is created. The focus of the coaching sessions is also sharpened as a result. The key questions that are addressed are: "What is your vision for the school?"; "What will you have achieved by the 100th day?"; "What kind of a leader do you want to be in this school?"; and "How will you know that you have achieved what you have set out to achieve?" Generally speaking, this coaching agreement can include a number of face-to-face or Skype coaching sessions (usually 4–6) and some e-mail communication in between sessions.

Aspiring school leaders can also benefit from coaching support. This can be one way of encouraging more potential leaders to consider becoming principals. Sometimes, independent support from an external coach can provide an aspiring leader with an opportunity to explore possibilities and ideas that it might be difficult to discuss with her own principal. Some training and development programs for aspiring school leaders include executive coaching sessions for their participants. For example, UK-based educational charity, Ambition School Leadership (https://www.ambitionschoolleadership.org .uk) incorporates coaching in their training programs as does the Leadership Diploma of Education in Denmark (Schleicher, 2012). These coaching sessions are delivered mainly by former or experienced school leaders. Such initiatives are supported by research. For example, a U.S. study showed that feedback *with coaching* made it more likely that principals would change their professional practices rather than feedback alone (Goff, Goldring, Guthrie, & Bickman, 2014).

Leaders Learning to Become Coaches

Another effective way to impact on educational leadership is to train principals to *become* coaches themselves. In an important text that had a significant role in the development of the field of coaching in education, *Leading Coaching in Schools*, there is a very strong message that leaders interested in introducing coaching into their institutions should develop *themselves* first (Creasy & Paterson, 2005, p. 10). Interestingly, the Centre for the Use of Research and Evidence in Education (2005) proposed that learning to become a coach or mentor was one of the most effective ways for leaders to become excellent practitioners. So not only does learning to become a coach support principals to introduce or embed coaching within their institutions, but it is suggested that it can also lead to improvements in their role as leaders. In a recent study, educators who undertook a coaching skills course reported that this led to insights about their own behaviors and relationship, suggesting that such training can be developmental beyond the course content (Barr & van Nieuwerburgh, 2015). Indeed, there may be multiple benefits in having school leaders who are trained coaches (see box).

IN CONTEXT: Possible Benefits of Having School Leaders Who Are Trained Coaches

- Coaching can be used to maintain energy and motivation in oneself and in others.
- Training to become a coach encourages reflective practice and self-development.
- Coaching skills are transferrable, allowing a principal to use these skills in her role as leader.
- School leaders will be able to provide coaching support to future and aspiring leaders within their organizations and elsewhere.
- Coaching processes can be helpful for managing meetings, professional development events, and training days.
- Feedback can be provided using a coaching approach.
- School leaders would be leading by example, encouraging more people within the organization to adopt coaching practices.

So the Educational Leadership portal focuses on providing leaders with access to coaching or building their coaching skills. In both ways, the quality of educational leadership can be improved with immediate and positive effects on the whole school community.

PROFESSIONAL PRACTICE

The second portal that we consider here is *coaching for professional practice*. This refers to the use of coaching to improve the capabilities, performance and well-being of staff within educational organizations. This includes the pedagogy and teaching practices of educators. While it is right that many school districts and authorities focus very clearly on the performance and well-being of their students, it must be acknowledged that the performance and well-being of educators is equally important. Broadly speaking, coaching to improve professional practice can take the form of teachers supporting one another or providing follow-up for educators and other school-based staff who have been on training programs.

Teachers Supporting Each Other

Educators working with one another to improve their teaching practice is a cost-effective and mutually supportive way of delivering professional development that helps build a collegial culture. Through the Kansas Coaching Project, Dr. Jim Knight (2007) has undertaken significant research into effective ways of improving teaching practice through coaching. Instructional coaching has been used widely across the United States and provides an evidence-based approach to supporting teachers to perform better in classrooms. In this approach, the instructional coach shares evidence-based teaching practices with her coachee (Knight & van Nieuwerburgh, 2012). These practices are discussed and agreed between the coach and the coachee before they are implemented in the classroom. While the instructional coach must be an expert in certain teaching practices, and is often required to demonstrate them to the coachee, the relationship between the coach and the coachee is characterized by a certain set of "partnership principles" (Knight, 2007). Knight (2007) argues that these principles are necessary to respect the professionalism of teachers (pp. 41–51).

The term *peer coaching* is used in other contexts to denote a reciprocal relationship between two colleagues (Foltos, 2013; Robbins, 2015; Robertson, 2008). In this case, both educators can be peers with neither one required to be an expert in specific teaching practices. In peer coaching, teachers work together to discuss areas of development that might lead to improvements in classroom practice. Usually, the teachers plan lessons together or decide on changes to classroom practice. This is followed by the new practice being trialed in the classroom before reconvening to reflect and evaluate the success of the lesson plan or new practice. Peer coaching is one way of providing cost-effective support for educators to improve teaching practice in classrooms (Kidd, 2009). It is also suggested that such approaches can enhance the development and well-being of both partners (Robertson, 2008).

Both approaches provide nonthreatening, tailored support to teachers that can lead to tangible improvements in classroom practice. Furthermore, such coaching interventions aim to respect the professionalism of educators and encourage experimentation in the classroom with the intention of improving teaching and learning.

Follow-Up for Educators and Other School-Based Staff

Another effective use of coaching within this portal is to provide support for educators and other school-based staff who have attended professional learning events. While 1-day or shorter courses for educators seem time effective, there is growing recognition that such professional development is not leading to significant improvements in the classroom. In fact, it has been argued that "one-shot" workshops can be counterproductive, leading to feelings of frustration when teachers find that they are unable to implement what they have learned on short courses that they may have been mandated to attend (Knight, 2000). Following a review of the academic literature, Cornett and Knight (2009) concluded that traditional training methods did not lead to changes in classroom practice. Knight (2012) subsequently refers to the "failure of traditional professional development" as a reason for introducing coaching into educational settings. Seminal work by Joyce and Showers (1995) showed that coaching can increase implementation of practices learned on training days. This is supported by later research by Shidler (2008) who finds that coaching educators about their teaching methods can have a direct positive impact on student achievement. All this suggests that providing coaching to educators who have attended training or professional development programs can be an effective way of leveraging the investment of time, making it more likely that these educators will think of ways to introduce the new learning into their everyday practice. This process can be inclusive of administrative and support staff who may be introducing new technologies, strategies, or ways of working.

WIDER SCHOOL COMMUNITY

While the idea of using coaching to create connections with the wider school community is appealing and has received attention recently, it is relatively under-researched (van Nieuwerburgh & Campbell, 2015). The term *wider school community* includes parents, caregivers, community leaders, and other stakeholders who can impact positively on the learning experiences of students. It is included in the Global Framework for two reasons. First, through practice, it has been realized that while providing coaching initiatives within schools can improve the experience of learners when they are on the premises, this is not always sustained when students return to their homes or community. Second, coaching interventions and approaches have the potential to develop and improve the ways in which schools connect with important stakeholders. This can be done in a number of ways. Below, we consider the ideas of training parents in coaching skills and teachers using a coaching approach when interacting with members of the wider school community.

Parents as Coaches

One approach that has been considered successful is providing parents and caregivers of students with coaching-related skills. Some schools have developed their own "parent as coach" programs in which school-based staff provide parents with coaching experiences or skills training. Parents who receive coaching skills training have reported better relationships with their children and an improved ability to support their learning (Bamford, Mackew, & Golawski, 2012). Such training can support parents by giving them an insight into coaching approaches and building their own confidence (Golawski, Bamford, & Gersch 2013; Wilson, 2011).

Using a Coaching Approach

In addition to imparting coaching skills to parents and caregivers, some educators are finding that using a coaching approach during parent conferences and parents' evenings improves communication. Some teachers find interactions with some parents difficult. The use of a coaching approach may improve relationships between teachers and parents, especially if the shared interests of all parties (the success and well-being of the student) can be established at the start of any interaction.

Although further research is evidently required, we believe that there is merit in using coaching approaches to build a sense of community around schools and improve relationships between parents and teachers.

COACHING FOR STUDENT SUCCESS AND WELL-BEING

While it is hoped that coaching-related interventions in any of the portals of the Global Framework will ultimately lead to improvements in student success and well-being, this portal focuses directly on this outcome. It is now widely accepted that providing coaching directly to students can have positive results (Devine et al., 2013).

Research has shown that students can derive various benefits from being coached. In one study in the UK, 16-year-old students received coaching over a three-year period. Compared to students who did not receive coaching, there was improved examination performance and increased levels of hopefulness (Passmore & Brown, 2009). A couple of studies based in Australian schools found that coaching provided by school-based staff led to increases in student resilience, well-being, and hopefulness (Campbell & Gardner, 2005; Green, Grant, & Rynsaardt, 2007). In another interesting study from Australia, teachers coached eleventh-grade students. This resulted in increases in academic goal-striving (Green Norrish, Vella-Brodrick, & Grant, 2013). Two more recent studies from England suggest that coaching can have a positive impact on young people categorized as "at risk" (Pritchard & van Nieuwerburgh, 2016; Robson-Kelly & van Nieuwerburgh, 2016). Overall, the growing body of research gives us reason to be hopeful about the effects of providing coaching directly to students in our schools.

It appears that there are also benefits for students who coach *others*. In a few important studies, it has been shown that students who are trained to become coaches (and subsequently coach other students) enhance their communication skills, improve their problem-solving abilities, and demonstrate increased confidence in finding solutions (van Nieuwerburgh, Zacharia, Luckham, Prebble, & Browne, 2012). In a related mixed methods study, 17- to 18-year-old high school students were trained to become coaches. After the newly trained student coaches had coached other students in their school, the study showed increases in their Emotional Intelligence scores. The newly trained student coaches also reported improvements in their study skills, self-confidence, communication skills, and relationships with others (van Nieuwerburgh & Tong, 2013).

Coaching can even have positive effects on elementary age children (Briggs & van Nieuwerburgh, 2012). In an earlier study, Briggs and van Nieuwerburgh (2010) showed that elementary school children could learn some peer coaching skills, even at the ages of 9 to 11. In a follow-up study, children were able to reflect on the reasons that they were more likely to accept feedback from some people rather than others (Dorrington & van Nieuwerburgh, 2015). Although the use of coaching in elementary school settings requires further research, initial findings are encouraging.

CONCLUSION

We have now surveyed the four portals of the Global Framework for Coaching in Education. We hope that this has provided a helpful conceptual playing field and context. In our experience of working in and with schools in different parts of the world, we believe that many of these initiatives can have a significant positive impact on student attainment, teacher well-being, and the school culture. As an educational leader, your engagement with coaching will play an important role in defining the school's culture. This Global Framework can provide a coherent way of thinking about, talking about, enhancing, and implementing various coaching initiatives in your school context.

SMALL STEP STARTER

At this stage, it may be helpful to understand what you hope to achieve by reading this book. Please take a moment to start a learning journal to capture your thoughts as you read. Jot down your answers to the questions below before getting into the next chapter.

- What do you hope to learn by reading this book?
- What would convince you that reading this book was a good investment of your time?
- What is your current view of coaching?
- How would you define "coaching in education" in one sentence?
- What type of leader are you striving to be?
- What type of leader does your school require?

REFERENCES

Australian Institute for Teaching and School Leadership. (2016). *Coaching and mentoring toolkit*. Retrieved from http://www.toolkit.aitsl.edu.au/category/coaching-mentoring

Bamford, A., Mackew, N., & Golawski, A. (2012). Coaching for parents: Empowering parents to create positive relationships with their children. In C. van Nieuwerburgh (Ed.), *Coaching in education: Getting better results for students, educators, and parents* (pp. 133–152). London, UK: Karnac.

Barr, M., & van Nieuwerburgh, C. (2015). Teachers' experiences of an introductory coaching training workshop in Scotland: An interpretative phenomenological analysis. *International Coaching Psychology Review, 10*(2), 190–204.

Briggs, M., & van Nieuwerburgh, C. (2010). The development of peer coaching skills in primary school children in years 5 and 6. *Procedia—Social and Behavioral Sciences, 9*, 1415–1422.

Briggs, M., & van Nieuwerburgh, C. (2012). Coaching in primary or elementary schools. In C. van Nieuwerburgh (Ed.), *Coaching in education: Getting better results for students, educators and parents* (pp. 47–61). London, UK: Karnac.

Campbell, J. (2016). Coaching in schools. In C. van Nieuwerburgh (Ed.), *Coaching in Professional Contexts*. London, UK: SAGE.

Campbell, M. A., & Gardner, S. (2005). A pilot study to assess the effects of life coaching with Year 12 students. In M. Cavanagh, A. M. Grant, & T. Kemp (Eds.), *Evidence-based coaching: Volume 1. Theory, research and practice from the behavioural sciences* (pp. 159–169). Bowen Hills, Queensland: Australian Academic Press.

Centre for the Use of Research and Evidence in Education. (2005). *National framework for coaching*. London, UK: CUREE.

Cornett, J., & Knight, J. (2009). Research on coaching. In J. Knight (Ed.), *Coaching: Approaches and perspectives* (pp. 192–216). Thousand Oaks, CA: Corwin.

Creasy, J., & Paterson, F. (2005). *Leading coaching in schools*. Nottingham, UK: NSCL.

Department for Education and Skills. (2003). Sustaining improvement: A suite of modules on coaching, running networks and building capacity. London, UK: Authors.

Dorrington, L., & van Nieuwerburgh, C. (2015). The development of peer coaching skills in primary school children: An exploration of how children respond to feedback. *International Journal of Information and Education Technology, 5*(1), 50–54.

Foltos, L. (2013). *Peer coaching: Unlocking the power of collaboration.* Los Angeles, CA: Corwin.

Goff, P., Goldring, E., Guthrie, J. E., & Bickman, L. (2014). Changing principals' leadership through feedback and coaching. *Journal of Educational Administration, 52*(5), 682–704.

Golawski, A., Bamford, A., & Gersch, I. (2013). *Swings and roundabouts: A self-coaching workbook for parents and those considering becoming parents.* London, UK: Karnac.

Green, L. S., Grant, A. M., & Rynsaardt, J. (2007). Evidence-based life coaching for senior high school students: Building hardiness and hope. *International Coaching Psychology Review, 2*(1), 24–32.

Green, L. S., Norrish, J. M., Vella-Brodrick, D. A., & Grant, A. M. (2013). Enhancing well-being and goal striving in senior high school students: Comparing evidence-based coaching and positive psychology interventions. *Institute of Coaching, Breaking Research, Scientific Findings from Harnisch Grant Recipients.*

James-Ward, C. (2013). The coaching experience of four novice principals. *International Journal of Mentoring and Coaching in Education, 2*(1), 21–33.

Joyce, B., & Showers, B. (1995). *Student achievement through staff development: Fundamentals of school renewal* (2nd ed.). White Plains, NY: Longman.

Kidd, W. (2009). Peer coaching and mentoring to improve teaching and learning. *Practical Research for Education, 42,* 50–55.

Knight, J. (2000, April). *Another damn thing we've got to do: Teacher perceptions of professional development.* Paper presented at the American Educational Research Association, New Orleans, LA.

Knight, J. (2007). Instructional coaching: A partnership approach to improving instruction. Thousand Oaks, CA: Corwin.

Knight, J. (2012). Coaching to improve teaching: Using the instructional coaching model. In C. van Nieuwerburgh (Ed.), *Coaching in education: Getting better results for students, educators, and parents* (pp. 93–113). London, UK: Karnac.

Knight, J., & van Nieuwerburgh, C. (2012). Instructional coaching: A focus on practice. *Coaching: An International Journal of Theory, Research and Practice, 5*(2), 100–112.

Passmore, J., & Brown, A. (2009). Coaching non-adult students for enhanced examination performance: A longitudinal study. *Coaching: An International Journal of Theory, Research and Practice, 2*(1), 54–64.

Pritchard, M., & van Nieuwerburgh, C. (2016). The perceptual changes in life experience of at-risk adolescent girls following an integrated coaching and positive psychology intervention group programme: An interpretative phenomenological analysis. *International Coaching Psychology Review, 11*(1), 57–74.

Robbins, P. (2015). *Peer coaching: To enrich professional practice, school culture, and student learning.* Alexandria, VA: Association for Supervision & Curriculum Development.

Robertson, J. (2008). *Coaching Educational Leadership: Building Leadership Capacity Through Partnership.* London: SAGE.

Robson-Kelly, L., & van Nieuwerburgh, C. (2016). What does coaching have to offer young people at risk of developing mental health problems? A grounded theory study. *International Coaching Psychology Review, 11*(1), 75–92.

Scottish College for Educational Leadership. (2016). *SCEL framework for educational leadership.* Retrieved from http://www.scelframework.com

Schleicher, A. (Ed.). (2012). *Preparing teachers and developing school leaders for the 21st century: Lessons from around the world.* Paris, France: OECD Publishing.

Shidler, L. (2008). The impact of time spent coaching for teacher efficacy on student achievement. *Early Childhood Educational Journal, 36*(5), 453–460.

van Nieuwerburgh, C. (2017). *An introduction to coaching skills: A practical guide* (2nd ed.). London, UK: SAGE.

van Nieuwerburgh, C. (Ed.). (2012). *Coaching in education: Getting better results for students, educators and parents*. London, UK: Karnac.

van Nieuwerburgh, C., & Barr, M. (2017). Coaching in education. In T. Bachkirova, G. Spence, & D. Drake (Eds.), *The SAGE Handbook of Coaching* (pp. 505–520). Thousand Oaks, CA: SAGE.

van Nieuwerburgh, C., & Barr, M. (Eds.). (2016). *Resources for coaching in education: Useful research and references*. Sydney, Australia: Growth Coaching International.

van Nieuwerburgh, C., & Campbell, J. (2015). A global framework for coaching in education. *CoachEd: The Teaching Leaders Coaching Journal, February 2015*, 2–5.

van Nieuwerburgh, C., & Tong, C. (2013). Exploring the benefits of being a student coach in educational settings: A mixed method study. *Coaching: An International Journal of Theory, Research and Practice, 6*(1), 5–24.

van Nieuwerburgh, C., Campbell, J., & Knight, J. (2015). Lesson in progress. *Coaching at Work, 10*(3), 35–37.

van Nieuwerburgh, C., Zacharia, C., Luckham, E., Prebble, G., & Browne, L. (2012). Coaching students in a secondary school: A case study. In C. van Nieuwerburgh (Ed.), *Coaching in education: Getting better results for students, educators, and parents* (pp. 191–198). London, UK: Karnac.

Wilson, A. (2011). How to be a parent champion and add magic to your family. Maidstone, UK: Every Family Matters.

Visit **www.growthcoaching.com.au** for more coaching and professional learning resources for educators.

CHAPTER 2

What Is Leadership Coaching?

In this chapter, we address a question that is of key importance to educational leaders: What is meant by the term *leadership coaching*? As we have argued already, confusion around terminology can make discussions about *coaching in education* quite difficult. For example, the use of coaching in a sports context describes a type of intervention that is quite different to the way it is used in educational settings. Further, one-to-one academic tutoring is also sometimes labeled *coaching*. Neither of these usages is consistent with how we define *coaching in education*.

Differences and similarities with other "helping conversations" like "mentoring," "instructing," and "counseling" have created uncertainty about what constitutes effective practice in these fields. In the previous chapter, we provided a definition of coaching (see Chapter 1). We believe that it is important for coaches to be clear about what they are doing, what kind of professional learning is being undertaken, and what is being investigated by researchers. For example, unless there is definitional clarity about *coaching* it can be difficult to know just what kind of learning conversation might take place or what research studies are describing. In this context, an essential requirement for successful outcomes within a school community is a shared understanding of the term *coaching*. This chapter clarifies what is meant by the term *leadership coaching* and explores the differences between *coaching* and a *coaching approach*.

WHAT IS LEADERSHIP COACHING?

In some contexts, *leadership coaching* refers to a coaching intervention that is designed specifically for leaders or aspiring leaders with the intention of developing the leadership capabilities of those participating. To be precise, the term is sometimes used to refer to coaching that is specifically focused on leadership capability, while at other times, it is a generic phrase relating to any coaching made available to people in leadership positions. This is how the term is typically understood within corporate contexts (Passmore, 2015).

In this book, we use the term *leadership coaching* to describe the range of coaching conversations, both formal and informal, that a leader may engage in with various team members and other stakeholders.

IN CONTEXT: Characteristics of Leadership Coaching

Leadership coaching:

- Incorporates some of the key elements of coaching.

- Involves two people in dialogue exploring a topic in which one person would like a different outcome.

- Is undertaken by someone in a leadership role.

- Can be an agreed formal conversation that is part of a series of meetings over time.

- Can also be a less formal, one-off conversation that takes place in a casual setting.

It is likely that *leadership coaching* will look, on the outside, like any other coaching conversation. There will be a significant amount of good listening, there will be many questions that provoke thinking and insight, there will be attempts to clarify what is wanted so that goals can be determined, and there will be exploration of options and identification of next steps. At the same time, some key dimensions distinguish *leadership coaching* from other types of coaching. The most significant differentiator of leadership coaching is the issue of power. The leadership coach comes to the coaching relationship in a more powerful place in the organizational hierarchy and in a position to have positive or negative influence on the coachee. The leadership coach, however highly skilled, is at a slight *disadvantage* in the coaching context compared with coaching that might be provided by a peer, since a power differential is present. The fact that the leadership coach has more perceived power in the organization than the person being coached inevitably influences the dynamics of the coaching relationship. Managing this power differential will have an important influence on how helpful and effective the coaching conversation will be.

It could be argued that power issues are present in any coaching relationship since simply adopting a coachee role puts oneself in a less powerful position than the coach. Organizational development consultant Edgar Schein (2009) explores this power issue and gives considerable attention to the topic describing the "One downness" of asking for help and the "One upness" of being asked for help: "[A]t the beginning, every helping relationship is in a state of imbalance. The client is one down and therefore vulnerable; the helper is one up and therefore powerful" (p. 39).

Schein (2009) goes further outlining some of the subtle traps that both a coachee and a coach can be drawn into as a result of this imbalance. The existence of these traps can negatively impact the effectiveness of the *helping* and therefore need to be acknowledged and managed. For the coachee, these traps include mistrust, looking for reassurance, and dependency. For the coach, the traps include advising, accepting the dependency, or inappropriately giving support (Schein, 2009). The leader and coachee relationship is made more complex by issues of responsibility and accountability when the leader is the school principal. In this situation, principals, more so than other leaders in the school, need to consider not only the needs of students and parents but also the needs of school councils and the wider school system in which they operate. The leadership coach needs to negotiate and manage the subtle power dynamics that exist in every helping relationship while also being aware of the more explicit power differential that comes from being a school principal.

IN DEPTH: Power in Relationship

The *Relational Teacher* (Loe, 2015) explores the role of power and its impact on relational quality. This text builds on a model of Relational Proximity originally proposed by Michael Schluter (1993). The Relational Proximity framework argues that *Parity* (how power is exercised and how differences in power are minimized) will be one of the key factors that influence the level of relational closeness (*Proximity*) that develops. Other factors within this framework influencing relational closeness include: *Directness*—the amount of direct communication; *Continuity*—the amount of shared contact over time; *Multiplexity*—the breadth of knowledge of each other, and *Commonality*—the extent of common interests, values, and goals. Schluter (1993) suggests strategies in which the power differences can be minimized, if not eliminated. All these suggestions describe ways in which the coach can take steps to minimize any formal differences in power. Incidentally, they also help manage the more nuanced power dynamics outlined by Schein above. In each instance, it is the person in the more powerful position who needs to explicitly initiate the actions that lead to minimizing the differences in power.

Strategies include:

- Openly acknowledging any hierarchical differences and agreeing how these differences will be managed
- Listening more than speaking

(Continued)

(Continued)

- Being fully present

- Explicitly clarifying roles for both coach and coachee

- Explicitly discussing the issue of confidentiality

- Agreeing what will happen with any written notes that might emerge from the conversations

- Meeting in a neutral venue

- Arranging any furniture so as to minimize any power differences

- Inviting feedback about the conversation

So can a leader effectively coach someone they supervise? Yes, it is possible if one recognizes the additional complexities. In this type of coaching, the power differential should be acknowledged, made explicit, and actively managed.

WHAT IS THE DIFFERENCE BETWEEN "COACHING" AND A "COACHING APPROACH"?

We have defined coaching as

a one to one conversation focused on the enhancement of learning and development through increasing self-awareness and a sense of personal responsibility, where the coach facilitates the self-directed learning of the coachee through questioning, active listening and appropriate challenge in a supportive and encouraging climate. (van Nieuwerburgh, 2012, p. 17)

By way of contrast we define using a coaching approach as *intentionally utilizing some of the transferable elements of formal coaching in a range of conversational situations that would not typically be considered coaching interactions.* If this is the case, then what are the transferable elements of coaching that can be transferred to a coaching approach? Based on our definition, coaching conversations contain the following dimensions:

- They focus on learning, growing self-awareness and awareness of others

- They encourage personal responsibility

- They are two-way conversations

- They focus on the coachee's agenda

- They encourage self-direction

- They provide both support and challenge

- They take place within an encouraging climate

- They are underpinned by a partnership approach

- They imply a nonevaluative stance by the coach

- They focus more on the present and the future (than the past)

When using a coaching approach, many of these dimensions remain present. A person may use a coaching approach in conversations where there are overt hierarchical differences in power, when in team conversations, in formal performance appraisal contexts, or when the coaching nature of the conversation has not been made explicit. None of these interactions would be considered typical coaching situations, but all can be enhanced by adopting a coaching approach.

IN CONTEXT: Adopting a Coaching Approach

When working with groups and teams, the process of goal setting and developing options and strategies to achieve identified goals can be just as helpful as it is during a one-to-one coaching conversation. The difference, of course, is that a group conversation is a much more complex conversation with many voices involved, more perspectives, and varying levels of trust (see Chapter 8 for a fuller exploration of this topic).

In formal appraisal processes, where an evaluative dimension exists, coaching as it has been defined is not possible. It is possible, however, to use key aspects of a coaching perspective such as effective questioning, good listening, goal setting, and a solution-focused approach in such a way that a much more effective appraisal results (see Chapter 6 for a fuller exploration of this topic).

These ways of operating can bring a significant difference to the way in which leaders might participate in a meeting, the way in which someone might respond to the knock on the door and the "Have you got a minute?" request, how a parent conference might be conducted, or how an interaction with a student in the playground might be shaped. All these conversations, where someone is wanting the current situation to be different and is willing to do something about it, can be enhanced by adopting a coaching approach.

Teacher:	"Can I have a moment to run something past you?"
Leader:	"Sure. I do have another meeting in just 10 minutes, so let's see how much we can do in that time and we can meet again later if we need to. Is that OK?"
Teacher:	"I've got this situation with . . ."
Leader:	"What's most on your mind about this?"
Teacher:	"Well . . ."
Leader:	"So what would you like to see happen here instead?"
Teacher:	"It would be great if . . ."
Leader:	"And what else would you be noticing if this situation was resolved . . . perfectly?"
Teacher:	"I would be noticing . . ."
Leader:	"And what else . . . ?"
Teacher:	"There would be . . ."
Leader:	"So you'd be noticing . . . and . . . and. . . . What would be the benefits of that?"
Teacher:	"It would just be so good to . . ."
Leader:	"So that's where you would like to get to on this? What's already happening that's helping you move in that direction?"
Teacher:	"Well, I guess . . ."
Leader:	"And what else? . . . And what else?"
Leader:	"So what would be a sign you were just a little bit closer to that ideal resolution of this?"
Teacher:	"A bit closer would mean . . ."
Leader:	"And what's one small action you can take toward that sign in the next 24 hours?"
Teacher:	"In the next 24 hours I can . . ."
Leader:	"Will you do that and let me know how you get on?"

NOTE: The idea of "Just-A-Minute conversations" were developed by Paul Jackson and Janine Waldman in *Positively Speaking: The Art of Constructive Conversations with a Solutions Focus*. See also the "Watch It in Practice" feature on page 22 for a video demonstration of a sample Just-A-Minute conversation using a coaching approach.

Although using a coaching approach is different from undertaking a formal coaching session, we propose that such conversations are enhanced because they

- Focus on helping to clarify an outcome
- Identify and explore resources and strengths that can assist in progress toward the outcome
- Explore options and strategies to help move toward what is wanted
- Generate insight and clarity through effective listening and questioning
- Help identify and commit to small next step actions
- Incorporate an element of accountability
- Demonstrate a supportive and encouraging approach from the leader

These coaching approach dimensions can be applied in almost any interaction where at least one person in the conversation would like a better outcome. It could be argued that the kind of approach outlined here and the skills required to bring a coaching approach to leadership are critical skills for leaders in complex adaptive systems. Recent publications focusing on leadership in corporate environments highlight the importance of the conversation as a significant component of effective leadership (Amabile & Kramer, 2011; Groysberg & Slind, 2012; McKergow & Bailey, 2015; Stanier, 2016). It can be argued that leadership is practiced through conversation. How leaders converse with team members, with clients, and with other stakeholders in one-to-one and one-to-group contexts will shape the nature of those interactions as well as their organizations. When organizations are viewed in this way, the use of coaching skills in various contexts take on significance, enabling people in organizations to move forward in helpful ways.

More recently, definitions of agile leadership (Breakspear, 2016; Heifetz, Grashow, & Linsky, 2009) either implicitly or explicitly give attention to the importance of the conversation. Prioritizing the conversational dimension of leadership highlights how useful the approach and skills of coaching can be for leaders in complex organizations. In this sense, we argue that all growth and development in the knowledge and skills of coaching supports effective leadership development.

CONCLUSION

In this chapter, we have provided a context-specific definition of leadership coaching. We have proposed that the use of a coaching approach by leaders can have a significant positive impact in schools. In our work, we argue for the inclusion of explicit teaching of coaching models, coaching skills, and techniques in leadership development programs for educators. We believe that coaching will increasingly be viewed as a critical skill of effective leadership.

While some aspects of the coaching approach discussed in this chapter have been included in leadership development programs for some time, bringing them into focus under the banner of a coaching approach gives them greater intentionality and focus.

EXPLORE FURTHER

- To learn more about using a coaching approach, read Stanier's *The Coaching Habit*.

- To learn more about Just-A-Minute conversations, read Jackson and Waldman's *Positively Speaking*.

- To learn more about power differences in helping relationships, read Schein's *Helping*.

SMALL STEP STARTER

In the coming weeks, make a point to notice when people discuss a topic or challenge regarding what they *don't* want to see happening. Most people are quite good at doing this.

If appropriate, invite them to think about what they might want to see happening instead: "So what would you like instead of all that?"

For example, a colleague might be expressing a concern about a lack of parental involvement in some school activity.

> "It's really disappointing the response that we get from parents on this. They don't seem to value this or really understand it or even take much interest to get behind what we are doing or to learn more about this project."

> "So what would you like instead of all that?" and/or "If this situation with parents was really working as you would like, what would you be noticing?"

Notice the response. It is not always easy for people to respond to this question, and it can seem quite confronting at times. We believe that a simple invitation to flip from "what's not wanted?" to "what's wanted instead?" is one small example of a key element of coaching—helping people focus on a positive outcome—can be introduced in any number of conversations. The impact of this question might surprise you.

REFERENCES

Amabile, T., & Kramer, S. (2011). *The progress principle: Using small wins to ignite joy, engagement and creativity at work*. Boston, MA: Harvard Business Review Press.

Breakspear, S. (2016). *Agile implementation for learning: How adopting an agile mindset can help leaders achieve meaningful progress in student learning*. Occasional Paper 147. Melbourne, Australia: Centre for Strategic Education.

Groysberg, B., & Slind, M. (2012). *Talk Inc.: How trusted leaders use conversation to power their organizations*. Boston, MA: Harvard Business Review Press.

Heifetz, R. A., Grashow, A., & Linsky, M. (2009). *The practice of adaptive leadership: Tools and tactics for changing your organization and the world*. Boston, MA: Harvard Business Review Press.

Jackson, P. Z., & Waldman, J. (2011). *Positively speaking: The art of constructive conversations with a solutions focus*. St Albans, UK: Solutions Focus.

Loe, R. (Ed.). (2015). *The relational teacher*. Cambridge, UK: Relational Schools.

McKergow, M., & Bailey, H. (2015). *Host: Six new roles of engagement*. London, UK: Solutions Books.

Passmore, J. (Ed.). (2015). *Leadership coaching*. London, UK: Kogan Page.

Schein, E. H. (2009). *Helping: How to offer, give, and receive help*. San Francisco, CA: Berrett Koehler.

Schluter, M., Lee, D., & Schluter, L. (1993). *The R factor*. London, UK: Hodder & Stoughton. London, UK: Nicholas Brealey.

Stanier, M. B. (2016). *The coaching habit: Say less, ask more, and change the way you lead forever.* Toronto, Ontario, Canada: Box of Crayons Press.

van Nieuwerburgh, C. (Ed.). (2012). *Coaching in education: Getting better results for students, educators and parents*. London, UK: Karnac.

Visit **www.growthcoaching.com.au** for more coaching and professional learning resources for educators.

CHAPTER 3

The GROWTH Coaching System

Coaching has been growing in popularity over the last few decades and is now used across a broad range of professional settings (Bachkirova, Spence, & Drake, 2017; van Nieuwerburgh, 2016). The GROWTH Coaching System has been developed for use within educational settings. As an education-focused methodology, it is having significant positive impact in schools and colleges (Campbell, 2016a). This system weaves together several interdependent components, which are explained in this chapter.

The GROWTH Coaching System has been developed and refined over many years through a combination of practice, theory, and research. Practicality, accessibility, immediacy, and difference making have been fundamentally important principles that have governed the development of this coaching system.

WHAT ARE THE VARIOUS ELEMENTS OF THE GROWTH COACHING SYSTEM?

The core elements that contribute to this coaching system are the **GROWTH Model, the Eight Key Coaching Skills** and the **Coaching Way of Being**. These elements provide a strong and stable foundation on which to base both formal coaching and the informal coaching approach conversations referred to in Chapter 2. The system is underpinned by evidence-based theories and supported by documentation tools that encourage and help track sustainable change.

ELEMENT 1: THE GROWTH MODEL

A central component of this system is the GROWTH model. This simple framework provides an easy-to-apply, flexible structure to any coaching interaction. The process is made up of eight steps (see Figure 3.1).

FIGURE 3.1 The GROWTH Model

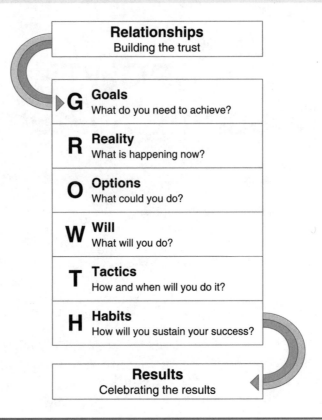

The GROWTH Model

- **Relationships** — Building the trust
- **G** — **Goals** — What do you need to achieve?
- **R** — **Reality** — What is happening now?
- **O** — **Options** — What could you do?
- **W** — **Will** — What will you do?
- **T** — **Tactics** — How and when will you do it?
- **H** — **Habits** — How will you sustain your success?
- **Results** — Celebrating the results

SOURCE: Campbell, J. (2016b). Framework for practitioners 2: The GROWTH model. In C. J. van Nieuwerburgh (Ed.), *Coaching in professional contexts* (pp. 235–240). London, UK: SAGE. © Growth Coaching International.

The GROWTH model can be considered a form of scaffolding that supports the coachee to explore ways of undertaking meaningful change. The idea of the scaffolding suggests that the model is similar to the temporary and often adaptable support structure on a construction site that enables a substantial building to emerge. Scaffolding provides an external frame necessary for the building to develop, particularly in the early stages; it initially overshadows the building but eventually recedes as the structure emerges. The scaffolding is never an end in itself but merely exists to enable the building to begin. Similarly, this model enables new insights and preferred futures to be created, implemented, sustained, and enjoyed. The GROWTH model is described in detail in Chapter 4.

ELEMENT 2: KEY COACHING SKILLS

Since coaching is, at its heart, a conversation, the skills that enable effective coaching are essentially interpersonal communication skills. Many people, especially educators, already demonstrate many of these skills, but in coaching contexts they are refined and nuanced in particular ways. For example, the skill of listening used in interpersonal interactions by most people all day and every day, is refined and deepened in ways that befit the more focused, purposeful, and respectful context of a coaching conversation. Similarly, questions used in a coaching context are less about seeking information and more about stimulating insights and awareness in the person being coached.

FIGURE 3.2 Eight Key Coaching Skills

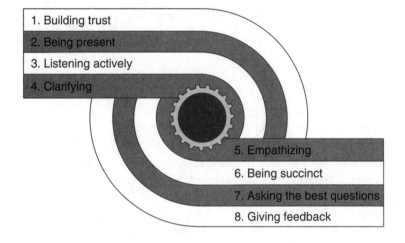

1. Building trust
2. Being present
3. Listening actively
4. Clarifying
5. Empathizing
6. Being succinct
7. Asking the best questions
8. Giving feedback

SOURCE: © Growth Coaching International.

Each of these eight communication skills permeate the various stages and steps in the GROWTH model (see Figure 3.2). Every one of the skills plays a role in weaving together the rich conversational "building" that develops. The use of these skills in a coaching context are outlined below.

1. Building Trust

Coaching conversations take place in a relationship—two people engaged in moving a topic forward in some way. It is the quality of this relationship that will impact what emerges. Trust is central to this coaching relationship. High levels of trust lead to relational safety, creativity, insight, and risk taking (Covey & Merrill, 2008). Therefore, it follows that low levels of trust may lead to doubts about whether the coaching relationship is worth continuing.

- Bring a curious, nonjudgmental approach.

- Maintain confidentiality.

- Demonstrate that you have the best interests of your coachee at heart.

- Do what you say you will do.

- Be open and honest.

- Be prepared to show vulnerability.

- Clarify expectations.

- Demonstrate your competence in the coaching process.

2. Being Present

Of all the coaching skills, it seems that being present has become the most difficult to master in recent times. Our contemporary world is one of stimulation and distraction, which sometimes work against the ability to provide full, focused attention in a coaching conversation. There are few greater gifts we can give another person these days than being present. When this is offered in abundance in coaching it makes a noticeable contribution to the quality of the thinking and insight that emerges. Further, since full and focused attention is so rare in our everyday conversational environments, it is also one of the most powerful ways to build trust.

3. Listening Actively

Closely related to providing full and focused attention is the ability to listen in ways that go beyond the conversational listening that dominates regular interactions. Listening at a level that really hears not only words but also emotions is enormously affirming, generating insights and self-understanding. Indeed, in coaching contexts it is more helpful that the focus of listening is in helping our coachees better understand themselves so that they can "own the issue," develop clarity, explore options, and move to action. Listening in a coaching context is not a quest for more information; rather, it is a process that enables your coachee to listen to herself, prompting growing awareness and insight.

4. Clarifying

Clarifying is a way of ensuring that the listening has worked. Clarifying consists of confirming that the coach has heard and understood what the coachee has said and intended. It may sound easy, but getting to shared meaning in most interactions involves more than someone making a statement and assuming that it has been received and understood in the same way that it was intended. Actively clarifying acknowledges these challenges and seeks to close any gaps in moving toward shared meaning. In coaching contexts, the clarifying process should be focused on the coachee (rather than the coach) gaining greater clarity.

COACHING TIPS: Being Present, Listening Actively, and Clarifying

- Make eye contact without staring.
- Prepare yourself to "be there" by avoiding obvious visible and audible distractions, phones, printers, others passing by, and so on.
- Write reminder notes that prompt you to redirect your attention whenever it might wander. These can be helpful as you prepare for coaching.
- Practice being present and listening in a focused way in *all* your interactions.
- Listen and notice patterns of language and expression.
- For some people, taking notes conveys a sense of focused attention. For others, note taking can cause anxiety. Check with your coachee and adapt your approach accordingly.
- Use your coachee's words in reflecting back to help them clarify.

5. Empathizing

Feeling heard is very affirming. In the clutter and noise of modern life it can be easy to be misheard or not heard at all. Being able to demonstrate empathy conveys the sense of "she gets it!" Knowing that someone gets your situation, even though that person may not necessarily agree with your position, is an important relational connector and provides a basis for moving forward. Without this sense of being heard and understood the coachee will feel compelled to convince and justify the current position, which can get in the way of attempts at moving forward.

COACHING TIPS: Empathizing

- Listen specifically for the emotional content.
- Develop your vocabulary of feeling words.
- Demonstrate that you are working at grasping their perspective by asking questions and explicitly seeking to confirm meaning.

6. Being Succinct

This is a more challenging coaching skill. As we have already argued, coaching is a self-directed learning experience in which the coachee does most of the thinking and talking, not a transfer of information from the coach to the coachee. In this context, it helps if the coach's verbal interventions are short, to the point, and add value.

COACHING TIPS: Being Succinct

- Focus on listening most of the time.
- Ask one question at a time.
- Be comfortable with silence to allow thinking time.
- Use short questions, "What else?" or question prompts such as "So . . . ?"

7. Asking the Best Questions

Skilled questioning is fundamental to impactful coaching. Coaches can use a variety of questions to support the thinking of their coachees. Open questions encourage exploration while closed questions can help the coachee to gain clarity. Mastering the subtle nuances of questioning in a coaching context takes practice and commitment but doing so will make the difference between average coaching and transformational coaching. "To question is to wield a powerful linguistic blade. It is necessary to ensure the blade is used to reveal strength and beauty rather than to carve away these same qualities" (McGee, Vento, & Bavelas, 2005, p. 382).

COACHING TIPS: Asking the Best Questions

- Use *What* questions frequently.
- Be careful with *Why* questions, because these can sometimes lead to defensiveness.
- Use open questions—"Can you say more about that?"
- Use closed questions—"When will you start on that?"
- Ask: "What else?" often.
- Questions that explore metaphors introduced by the coachee can be helpful. For example, if a coachee commented on an aspect of the current chapter of her career, a helpful question might ask about the title of the next chapter in her career.
- Direct your questions to resourceful areas: "How were you able to be so successful in that situation?"

8. Giving Feedback

Giving feedback is one of the skills of coaching that helps ensure that coaching conversations go beyond being merely pleasant social interactions. Skill in giving feedback is a critical part of helping the coachee gain greater insight and awareness about herself and the situation on which the coaching focuses. Feedback given and received well can enable significant growth and learning to occur. We discuss this topic in greater detail in Chapter 7.

Above, we have surveyed eight key coaching skills. Some of these are addressed in greater detail later in this book. Now, we turn our attention to the coaching way of being, one of the foundational elements of effective coaching.

ELEMENT 3: THE COACHING WAY OF BEING

Given the highly relational nature of coaching, how you "show up" in the coaching interaction is an important (if not the most important) component of the GROWTH Coaching System. The American philosopher Emerson once stated, "What you do speaks so loudly I can't hear what you say." This quote neatly highlights how the way in which we present ourselves in coaching interactions can have a significant influence on how the coaching relationship might unfold.

What Constitutes a Coaching Way of Being?

Practitioners have explored this area since the term *way of being* was first introduced by Carl Rogers (1995). We argue that a Coaching Way of Being includes a confluence of

> "If you change the conversation, then there's every chance you will change everything around it."
>
> —Paul Jackson and Janine Waldman, *Positively Speaking* (2011)

- qualities such as humility, curiosity, generosity;

- skills related to Emotional Intelligence;

- beliefs including positive regard for the coachee; belief in her ability to change and grow; and

- principles including partnership and respect.

This Coaching Way of Being provides the relational climate in which the models and tools of coaching can be introduced (see Figure 3.3). When safety and trust exist it is more likely that the coaching relationship will flourish and that your coachee will achieve the kinds of insight and growth that make the interaction satisfying for both parties. Interestingly, of all the skills and knowledge that effective coaches need to learn, the Coaching Way of Being is probably the most difficult.

FIGURE 3.3 The Coaching Way of Being

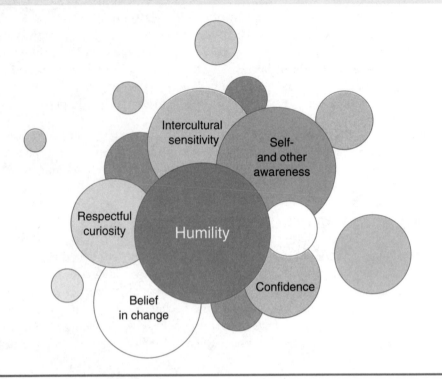

Intercultural sensitivity

Self- and other awareness

Respectful curiosity

Humility

Confidence

Belief in change

SOURCE: © Growth Coaching International.

How Might You Begin to Develop Your Coaching Way of Being?

Some of the more recently developed tools relating to exploring Emotional Intelligence (EI) (David, 2016; Freedman, 2007) can be helpful. While we would consider the Coaching Way of Being as more than simply EI, this framework helps make the topic tangible and accessible. More important, EI can provide a way into developing and growing in this area. In recent years, numerous workshops, websites, assessment tools, and books have been produced on this topic, and most of these are a helpful place to start when seeking to reflect on and enhance your Coaching Way of Being.

Further, commonly used personal profiling models can also play a role in helping people grow in self- and other awareness. Some commentators have asked challengingly, "Do you know what it is like to be on the other side of you?" (Kubicek & Cockram, 2015, p. 2). Profiling tools, especially those with a multi-rater component, can be helpful in providing a response to this question. Increasing self-awareness is a first step toward identifying development areas and working intentionally to refine and enhance effectiveness.

- Try to be aware of, and understand, your moods, emotions, and motivations as well as their effect on others. People often see a leader's emotional reaction as the most legitimate response and then model their own on it.

- Suspend judgment—think before acting. For instance, if you become annoyed by someone's actions, express your feelings by writing them down. Once you've recorded what has irritated you, list the ideal win-win outcome from your next communication with that person. Such a delayed response will help prevent you from saying something that you might later regret and give you the space to plan for a better outcome.

- Demonstrate empathy by treating people according to their emotional reactions. Sometimes it's too easy to get caught up in the task we want others to achieve and ignore how they are responding as individuals.

- Find common ground and build rapport with others. Take the time to inquire about other people's dreams and aspirations. Constantly focus on their needs, their wants, and their desires.

Above, we have presented the main components of the GROWTH Coaching System. We shared the GROWTH model and then identified the eight key skills of an effective coach. The Coaching Way of Being is also briefly explored. A few additional elements of the GROWTH Coaching System are discussed below.

THEORETICAL PERSPECTIVES UNDERPINNING THE GROWTH COACHING SYSTEM

While the System gives great emphasis to coaching tools that lead to practical outcomes, it is based on a solid theoretical footing. The interrelated fields of Appreciative Inquiry, Positive Psychology, and Positive Organizational Scholarship have emerged independently over the last 20 years or so. While there are some significant differences between these approaches, there are many points of intersection. Some of these common themes include an emphasis on

- exploring strengths rather than weaknesses;

- uncovering what is working rather than what is not working;

- giving more attention to exploring the desired future than focusing on problems in the past;

- hope, optimism, and a focus on the future;

- language and how it plays a part in shaping and reshaping perceptions; and

- small step approaches to change.

In recent years, the solution-focused approach has come to play an increasingly influential role within the GROWTH Coaching System (see Chapter 5).

It has been exciting to see emerging research that supports these strengths-based approaches. Many educators have intuitively recognized the importance of these concepts but it is only in recent times that empirical research has provided scientific support for these approaches (Biswas-Diener, 2010; Jackson & McKergow, 2002; Joseph, 2015; Macdonald, 2011; Orem, Binkert, & Clancy, 2007). For more detailed information on these perspectives, and the solution-focused approach in particular, see Chapter 5.

COACHING DOCUMENTATION

An important component of the GROWTH Coaching System is the documentation that records the goals, actions, and progress of the coaching process. Over the years, the value of recording goals and actions has proven to be a particularly helpful part of the formal coaching process. Committing goals and actions to written form achieves several things:

- It helps bring further clarity to the topics discussed.

- It provides evidence of commitments and helps build accountability into the coaching process.

> "It is often wonderful how putting down on paper a clear statement of a case helps one to see, not perhaps the way out, but the way in."
>
> —A. C. Benson

- It provides a way of clarifying and drawing together the various threads of the conversation at the end of the session into concise action points. This helps with keeping the coaching succinct.

- It provides evidence of progress. When formal coaching is reaching its conclusion, it is helpful to invite coachees to reflect on where they were in relation to various goals at the beginning of the coaching process. Without the opportunity to return to statements and ratings made weeks or months earlier, it is sometimes difficult for coachees to remember where they were when the coaching process began and therefore how much progress has been achieved.

- At a practical level, it provides a way for busy school leaders to keep all documents related to the coaching process—goal tracking, actions, handouts, feedback surveys, and so on in one place. More important, it helps provide a reminder of the coaching story that began in the first session.

- These ways of documenting progress in coaching can all be made more efficient, accessible, and faster via various software programs and apps. Some have been specifically designed for coaching, but any generally available electronic note-taking programs (e.g., Evernote or OneNote) can be used.

Watch It in Practice

A Typical Coaching Session

In this chapter, we have explored the model, skills, and way of being of coaching. Watch the video to see an example of a typical coaching session. It may be helpful to make some notes about the key skills and coaching way of being that you notice while watching the session.

resources.corwin.com/campbellcoaching

CONCLUSION

The GROWTH Coaching System is more than the sum of its various parts; each component interweaves with the others to provide a robust, flexible, theoretically sound, highly practical, and well-proven coaching methodology. The system has been widely used in schools and provides a way of making coaching and a coaching approach accessible, learnable, and usable. Since we believe that schools are conversational communities and that dialogue is a central component of change, conversations that are based on the elements outlined in the GROWTH Coaching System will help schools move toward becoming transforming communities.

EXPLORE FURTHER

- To learn more about other coaching conversation frameworks, read Whitmore's *Coaching for Performance*.

- To learn more about coaching skills, read van Nieuwerburgh's *An Introduction to Coaching Skills*.

- To learn more about Way of Being, read Rogers' *A Way of Being*.

- To learn more about developing Emotional Intelligence, read Bradberry and Greaves' *Emotional Intelligence 2.0* and Freedman's *At the Heart of Leadership*.

SMALL STEP STARTER

1. Coaching Way of Being: The Coaching Way of Being component of the Growth Coaching System can be challenging to explore but it is an influential factor in the approach. When the skills and the coaching framework are anchored in a human being whose coaching presence radiates warmth, authenticity, and a sense of "this person is here for me," then the coaching skills and tools are greatly enhanced.

   We can have blind spots in this area, however. As indicated above, various multi-rater and profile tools can help uncover Coaching Way of Being blind spots. Another simple way to develop in this Coaching Way of Being element is to invite feedback from close friends and colleagues.

   You can set this up by

   - Giving some context to the questions. For example, "I am an interested in exploring the way I come across as a coach in our coaching sessions, and I wonder whether you would be prepared to provide some feedback?"

   - Inviting comment on some of the key Coaching Way of Being concepts—"humility," "warmth," or demonstration of "partnering." Perhaps you might even provide a short written definition of the Coaching Way of Being, highlighting the key aspects about which you would like feedback.

2. Listening: The skill of listening is arguably the most important of all the key coaching skills in the GROWTH Coaching System. Being skilled in this area can also help develop your Coaching Way of Being. One strategy that will help you refine the way you listen is to focus on listening as a way to help the people you are listening to gain insights. Often we approach listening as a way of gaining information but in coaching it helps if our listening is focused on helping our coachees to listen to *themselves*.

   This week, in your regular interactions with others, make a point at different times to focus on listening to bring clarity to your colleagues or friends rather than listening for information for yourself. Notice what difference this shift in mindset might bring.

REFERENCES

Bachkirova, T., Spence, G., & Drake, D. (Eds.). (2017). *The SAGE handbook of coaching*. London, UK: SAGE.

Biswas-Diener, R. (2010). *Practicing positive psychology coaching: Assessment, activities, and strategies for success*. Hoboken, NJ: John Wiley & Sons.

Bradberry, T., & Greaves, J. (2009). *Emotional intelligence 2.0*. San Diego, CA: TalentSmart.

Campbell, J. (2016a). Coaching in Schools. In C. van Nieuwerburgh (Ed.), *Coaching in professional contexts* (pp.131–143). London, UK: SAGE.

Campbell, J. (2016b). Framework for practitioners 2: The GROWTH model. In C. van Nieuwerburgh (Ed.), *Coaching in professional contexts* (pp. 235–240). London, UK: SAGE.

Covey, S. M. R., & Merrill, R. R. (2008). *Speed of trust: The one thing that changes everything.* New York, NY: Simon & Schuster.

David, S. (2016). *Emotional agility: Get unstuck, embrace change and thrive in work and life.* New York, NY: Penguin.

Freedman, J. (2007). *At the heart of leadership: How to get results with emotional intelligence.* Freedom, CA: Six Seconds.

Jackson, P. Z., & McKergow, M. (2002). *The solutions focus: The SIMPLE way to positive change (people skills for professionals).* London, UK: Nicholas Brealey International.

Jackson, P. Z., & Waldman, J. (2011). *Positively speaking: The art of constructive conversations with a solutions focus.* St Albans, UK: Solutions Focus.

Joseph, S. (Ed.). (2015). *Positive psychology in practice: Promoting human flourishing in work, health, education, and everyday life.* Hoboken, NJ: John Wiley & Sons.

Kubicek, J., & Cockram, S. (2015). *5 gears: How to be present and productive when there is never enough time.* Hoboken, NJ: John Wiley & Sons.

Macdonald, A. (2011). *Solution-focused therapy: Theory, research and practice* (2nd ed.). London, UK: SAGE.

McGee, D., Vento, A. D., & Bavelas, J. B. (2005). An interactional model of questions as therapeutic interventions. *Journal of Marital and Family Therapy, 31*(4), 371–384.

Orem, S. L., Binkert, J., & Clancy, A. L. (2007). *Appreciative coaching: A positive process for change.* New York, NY: John Wiley & Sons.

Rogers, C. (1995). *A way of being.* Boston, MA: Houghton Miffin.

van Nieuwerburgh, C. (2017). *An introduction to coaching skills: A practical guide* (2nd ed.). London, UK: SAGE.

van Nieuwerburgh, C. (Ed.). (2016). *Coaching in professional contexts.* London, UK: SAGE.

Whitmore, J. S. (2009). *Coaching for performance: Growing human potential and purpose— the principles and practice of coaching and leadership* (4th ed.). Boston, MA: Nicholas Brealey.

Visit **www.growthcoaching.com.au** for more coaching and professional learning resources for educators.

CHAPTER 4

Applying the Eight-Step Coaching Model

The GROWTH model is central to the coaching approach outlined in this book (see Figure 4.1). This simple, versatile framework is an extension of the GROW model popularized by Sir John Whitmore (2009). It is relatively easy to learn so that you can apply it in coaching interactions in ways that make a positive difference. The key components of this model are outlined in detail in this chapter.

FIGURE 4.1   The GROWTH Model

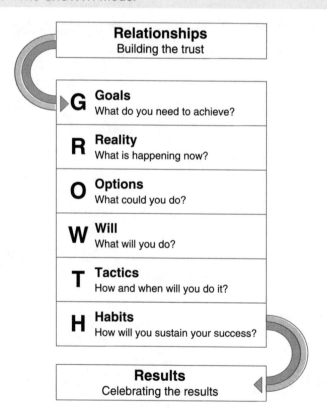

SOURCE: Campbell, J. (2016). Framework for practitioners 2: The GROWTH model. In C. van Nieuwerburgh (Ed.), *Coaching in professional contexts* (pp. 235–240). London, UK: SAGE. © Growth Coaching International.

STEP 1: BUILD TRUST

We believe that this is a foundational requirement for effective coaching conversations. Furthermore, trust is critical to positive relational climates within school contexts (Bryk & Schneider, 2004; Covey & Merrill, 2008). This is why the GROWTH process starts with a focus on the relationship. In practical terms, this means that the coach should prioritize the creation of a mutually respectful and trusting relationship at the start of a coaching interaction. Research in the field supports the view that the quality of a relationship is fundamental to the success of coaching interactions (De Haan, 2008).

STEP 2: GOALS—WHAT DO YOU NEED TO ACHIEVE?

Once trust has been established, the coach should find out what the coachee would like to achieve and whether she is prepared to commit to some actions to move toward this. It helps to establish a level of commitment to action as early as possible so that the coaching conversation has the best chance of success. Following this, the coach should help the coachee be clear about what she wants in relation to the opportunity or challenge in as much detail as possible.

COACHING TIPS: Sample "Goal" Questions

- What do you need to achieve? Tell me more about that.

- If we worked together on this regularly for the next 3 months, what would you like to have happen that is not happening now?

- What would be the result of that?

- How will that be of real value to you?

- What will be the benefits of achieving this goal? What will be the costs if you don't achieve this goal?

- When you achieve this goal, what will it look like and/or feel like?

- Is that realistic? Can we do that in the time we have available?

- What else? What else?

Setting Up the Goal

How you state the goal is very important, as are the number of goals. It may be helpful to keep the acronym ISMART in mind when establishing the goal (see Figure 4.2). This is based on the well-known SMART acronym first popularized in 1981 (Doran, Miller, & Cunningham).

SOURCE: © Growth Coaching International.

FIGURE 4.2 ISMART Goals

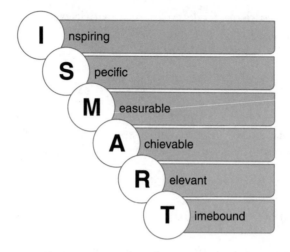

I—Inspiring

Does it make your coachee feel more satisfied, more confident, more challenged, more in control, and/or more like she is making a difference? Can she see the personal benefits of achieving this goal?

S—Specific

Is your coachee clear about what she wants to achieve? The more detail used in describing the preferred future the better. Detail serves to bring clarity and helps intensify motivation.

M—Measurable

How will your coachee know when the goal has been achieved? What would she be noticing?

A—Achievable

Is the goal reasonable, given past behaviors, existing attitudes, other commitments, the environment, and resources available? Is it sufficiently challenging to motivate the coachee? It is important to have some level of stretch but not so much that it undermines the chances of the coachee's success.

R—Relevant

Is this consistent with the school plan and priorities this year?

Is this relevant to the coachee's development priorities?

How does this goal relate to departmental priorities?

How passionate is the coachee about this goal?

T—Timebound

Is the time frame likely to build momentum without the coachee feeling unnecessarily pressured? Identifying a specific time in the future can help galvanize action and bring greater clarity and commitment.

Below is a helpful framework for stating goals:

By . . . (This helps establish the time frame.)

I am/have . . . (This section describes the details of the preferred future as if these things are already in place.)

So that . . . (This component prompts thinking about the benefits and the "why this is important" aspect of this preferred future, thereby making it more explicit.)

 IN CONTEXT: Examples of Goals

The goal may be something as simple as:

"By Friday my work space is tidy and organized so that I can find what I need."

Or the goal may be more long term:

"By the end of June I am producing student reports efficiently and easily due to my increased knowledge of spreadsheets."

Or the goal may be more far-reaching like:

"By the end of the year I have effectively implemented a peer coaching program so that people are committed and engaged and it is making a positive impact on the quality of teaching in our department."

The number of goals you focus on at a time will depend on the complexity of the goal and the time available to commit to working on the goals. The key is to select goal areas that will make a significant difference to success and well-being of your coachee. Sometimes it will also be important to consider the impact of the goal on the well-being and success of other people in the organization.

A Note of Caution About Goal Setting

Getting clear and specific about the preferred future in relation to a particular challenge or opportunity can bring focus and targeted actions to what might previously have been a vague, good intention. Schools are, however, complex organizations, and circumstances are likely to change. This means that working step by step, inflexibly and rigidly toward an outdated goal can be unhelpful. There is a risk that such an approach can lead to undue stress and a lack of awareness that circumstances have changed. In such situations, it helps if goals and strategies are regularly reviewed and open to being modified if necessary.

STEP 3: REALITY—WHAT IS HAPPENING NOW?

This stage of the coaching process allows your coachee to get clear about what is already in place that will facilitate the achievement of the goal. By this we mean the resources, skills, and strengths that are already there. This is not to say that conversations about things that are not going well are avoided altogether. However, coaches should be aware that focusing too much on what is not working can lead to a negative downward spiral. So while it is helpful to acknowledge deficiencies, it should be kept in mind that coachees are much more likely to become resourceful and motivated when talking about what is already working.

COACHING TIPS: Sample "Reality" Questions

- What do you already have in place that will help to increase the likelihood of your achieving this goal?

- How do you know this is accurate?

- When does this happen? Be precise if possible.

- What other factors are relevant?

(Continued)

(Continued)

- What is the perception of the situation?

- What have you tried so far? What's working?

- What else? What else?

- What's within your area of control?

- On a scale of 1–10 where 10 is the ideal outcome and 1 is the worst it has been, where are you now?

COACHING TIPS: Taking Notes

In formal or extended coaching conversations the coach may wish to take notes. In this case, it is important for the coach to ask for permission and to be transparent about how the notes will be used and stored. A coach should inform her coachee that the purpose of the notes is

- To assure her that the coach is totally present and focused on her needs

- To ensure that the coach has listened effectively

- For the coachee to clarify and/or expand on any important points as necessary based on the information fed back using the notes

COACHING TIPS: Tapping Into the Perceptions of Others

While it is very important to encourage the coachee to analyze her own perceptions of reality, the role of the coach is also to inspire and equip the coachee to research the perceptions of others. Ask:

- How would you view your current effectiveness in this situation?

- How would others view your effectiveness in this situation?

- What can you do to ensure that you have accurate feedback from others regarding how this is progressing?

STEP 4: OPTIONS—WHAT COULD YOU DO?

The role of a coach at this point is to help the coachee explore all the possible options for action that would enable her to achieve her goal.

COACHING TIPS: Sample "Option" Questions

- What are the options for achieving this goal?

- What could you do to change the situation? What alternatives are there to that approach? What else?

- What approaches have you used yourself, or seen others use, in similar circumstances?

- What are the benefits and pitfalls of these options?

COACHING TIPS: Encouraging New Thinking

Questions a coach could ask to promote thinking from a fresh perspective include:

- What is the opposite action to what you have been taking so far?

- What ideas/advice would you give others in your situation?

- What would you do if you *did* know what to do?

- Tell me two more options. And what else?

- Who do you know who would be able to confidently overcome this challenge? What would she do if she were in this situation?

STEP 5: WILL—WHAT WILL YOU DO?

Having explored the various possibilities, the coach now needs to assist the coachee to select the best options for action, given her present circumstances, to achieve her goal. For example the coach could ask, "Out of all these possibilities, which energizes you the most?" Often, following the positive energy "pathway" is a helpful way to create momentum.

- What options do you like the most for action during the coming week?

- What will you do, specifically?

- What are the next steps?

STEP 6: TACTICS—HOW AND WHEN WILL YOU DO IT?

Now the coach is moving the coachee to real and practical action. The coach plays an important role in helping the coachee commit to following through by encouraging her to picture the details of the action she will be taking. Small step actions that progress the situation are important here, not large-scale action plans. Tactics are best when they are small steps that can take place within the next 24 hours or so. Getting started and creating momentum are important at this point.

- How and when will you do it?

- Precisely when will you take the next steps?

- Do you need to log the steps in your diary?

- What is the next small step to progress this option?

In formal coaching it is helpful to record actions in writing. It is another step toward turning the invisible into the visible because it increases clarity, commitment, confidence, and accountability. It's a good idea for both the coach and the coachee to record the agreed actions toward the end of each session.

During follow-up sessions it can be helpful to invite reflection on the impact of the agreed actions. A coach might ask a question such as: "What are two lessons that you learned from taking this action?" These insights can even be recorded as a means of encouraging quality reflection. In this way, a journal that tracks the learning journey begins to emerge.

STEP 7: HABITS—HOW WILL
YOU SUSTAIN YOUR SUCCESS?

Through coaching conversations, a coachee is able to leverage and create positive, empowering habits. One way a coach can facilitate this process is by affirming strengths or qualities that the coachee might already be demonstrating. The coach might make some notes during the conversation to aid with this. Another strategy would be to ask the coachee to identify an existing quality that will support her in achieving success. Raising the coachee's awareness of the range of physical and human resources available to support her is one of the key tasks of the coach. In informal coaching conversations, one of the most powerful yet simple forms of support is for one person to take an active interest in when and how the other will complete the action. For example, the question "How would it be if we met after you have taken these actions so you can tell me how things went for you?" can increase motivation and commitment to action.

COACHING TIPS: Sample "Habit" Questions

- How will you ensure that you carry out these actions?

- What support and/or structures are needed to maintain this? What else?

- What needs to be different about your thoughts, feelings, behaviors, or environment to ensure you carry out these actions?

- What might get in the way? How can we address that?

- What sort of person do you need to be to achieve the results you desire?

- What different attitudes/values/beliefs will be helpful?

STEP 8: RESULTS—
CELEBRATING THE RESULTS

The key at this stage is to help the coachee acknowledge her efforts and achievements. The focus of this part of the conversation is to identify successes to celebrate. The following coaching questions promote self-reflection and provide permission to explicitly acknowledge strengths and achievements.

- What did you do to surprise yourself?

- What strengths did you uncover here that might be helpful elsewhere?

- What do you wish to acknowledge yourself for?

- How will you celebrate your success?

IN CONTEXT: Using GROWTH Within a Leadership Coaching Approach

In Chapter 2, we explored the differences and similarities between coaching and using a coaching approach. One key difference is the power differential that exists between a leader and her colleague. Much of the coaching skills and the GROWTH model will still apply. However, there may be slight differences:

- Using a coaching approach may mean that a leader is more directive in identifying goal areas and in shaping specific goals because of an organizational responsibility to the development of colleagues in the organization. It is important that ownership of goals and responsibility for taking action to achieve them is maintained with the colleague.

- In developing options in the GROWTH process, it can be helpful at times to assist in the generation of possible strategies by asking, "Would you like suggestions from me?" Though the focus is primarily on helping the colleague self-generate possibilities, it can be appropriate to ask this question. Some caveats:

  - Options should be presented as an extension of the list developed by the colleague.

  - Be aware that any suggestions provided by a leader may be perceived as the "right answer" by colleagues.

- Offering possible additional options can help get the brainstorming of possibilities unstuck and provide a perspective on the topic that triggers more and different ideas.

- The use of coaching notes is significant in this context because they are much more likely to be seen as record-keeping than as a constructive tool in the coaching process. Consequently, if notes are taken it is important for transparency about how notes will be used and stored.

- It is also important by this stage of the coaching process to be aware of practical ways that the leader might be able to take responsibility for addressing legitimate concerns that a colleague may have shared during the conversation. The leader should consider the following question: "Am I or this organization inhibiting my colleague's progress through:
  - Limiting organizational structures?
  - Creating contradictory priorities?
  - Providing insufficient resources?
  - Long established and limiting patterns of behavior between my colleague and myself?"

Watch It in Practice

The GROWTH Process

In this chapter, we have focused on the eight steps of the GROWTH model. Watch the full-length coaching session to see an example of the GROWTH process in action. It may be helpful to make notes about the various steps that you notice during the conversation.

resources.corwin.com/campbellcoaching

CONCLUSION

The GROWTH model is a tried and tested process that has brought clarity and energy to countless conversations. While we have necessarily presented the model in a linear way, it is not a rigid formula for coaching success. The movement toward unlocking opportunities or overcoming challenges rarely happens in a straight line. Things are changing all the time: understanding of the issues, of oneself, of circumstances, and so many other variables. Nevertheless, having access to a coaching framework such as GROWTH helps both experienced and new coaches effectively navigate conversations. Such a framework gives coaches confidence that they have a structure that supports the emergence of new insights and new actions. Ultimately, this will lead to improved performance, better relationships, and enhanced well-being.

EXPLORE FURTHER

- To learn more about using a coaching conversation framework, read Jackson and McKergow's *The Solutions Focus*.

- To learn more about GROWTH, read Campbell's "Framework for Practitioners 2: The GROWTH Model" in *Coaching in Professional Contexts*.

SMALL STEP STARTER

When you are next involved in an informal coaching conversation, spend more time than you might normally do teasing out details related to the goal. Help explore it in rich behavioral detail with these kinds of questions:

- What will *you* be noticing when this ideal scenario is in place? And what else?

- What will others be noticing? And what else?

- What will other key stakeholders be doing? And what else?

Use the "What else?" question to respectfully access more detail.

Notice what happens for the person you are coaching, and for yourself.

REFERENCES

Bryk, A. S., & Schneider, B. L. (2004). *Trust in schools: A core resource for improvement.* New York, NY: Russell Sage Foundation.

Campbell, J. (2016). Framework for practitioners 2: The GROWTH model. In C. van Nieuwerburgh (Ed.), *Coaching in professional contexts* (pp. 235–240). London, UK: SAGE.

Covey, S. M. R., & Merrill, R. R. (2008). *Speed of trust: The one thing that changes everything.* New York, NY: Simon & Schuster.

De Haan, E. (2008). *Relational coaching: Journeys towards mastering one-to-one learning.* The Atrium, Southern Gate, Chichester, West Sussex, UK: John Wiley & Sons.

Doran, G., Miller, A., & Cunningham, J. (1981). There's a S.M.A.R.T. way to write management goals. *Management Review, 70*(11), 35–36.

Jackson, P. Z., & McKergow, M. (2002). *The solutions focus: The SIMPLE way to positive change (people skills for professionals).* London, UK: Nicholas Brealey International.

Whitmore, J. S. (2009). *Coaching for performance: Growing human potential and purpose—the principles and practice of coaching and leadership* (4th ed.). Boston, MA: Nicholas Brealey.

CHAPTER 5

Positive, Strength-Based Approaches Underpinning the GCI Coaching System

In recent years, positive, strength-based approaches to organizational and personal change have expanded considerably in scope and influence (Boniwell, 2010; Hefferon & Boniwell, 2011; Seligman, 2002, 2011). The field of Positive Organizational Scholarship has been studying these concepts as they apply to organizations since 2003, with a particular focus on positive leadership (Cameron, Dutton, & Quinn, 2003). David Cooperrider pioneered appreciative approaches to change in organizations in the 1980s (Whitney, Trosten-Bloom & Cooperrider, 2010), and solution-focused practitioners have been employing positive, strength-based approaches in therapeutic contexts for over 30 years (Iveson, George, & Ratner, 2011; Jackson & McKergow, 2002; Shennan, 2014). Since these areas all explore ways to optimize human performance and well-being, they have much to offer the field of coaching.

SOLUTION-FOCUSED APPROACHES

The solution-focused (SF) perspective has its origins in the therapeutic approach developed by Insoo Kim Berg and Steve de Shazer (de Shazer, Korman, Berg, & Trepper, 2007). It is an approach that values simplicity and aims to discover "what works" in a given situation. Coaches using a solution-focused approach work with organizations and people drawing on a fundamental set of principles:

- It is not necessary to understand the cause of the problem to help people find a solution.

- Focusing on the future creates more useful energy than focusing on past problems.

- Every problem has exceptions.

- If something works, do more of it.

- If something does not work, then stop and try something different.

- Change comes from small steps.

- People are amazingly resourceful when you allow them to be. (Adapted from Greer, 2010)

The first principle (the idea that we do not need to understand the problem to find solutions) could be considered counter-intuitive. However, in schools, and other human intensive organizations, issues involving people do not always unfold in logical, predictable ways. If we are analyzing a problem with a machine, root cause problem solving is entirely appropriate. However, schools are complex human systems, so alternative approaches to exploring opportunities and challenges can be more helpful (O'Connor & Cavanagh, 2013).

The solution-focused approach invites us to minimize investigation of the problem and to maximize exploration of what is preferred in the future in relation to the topic or concern. It also gives more focus to what is already working. When adopting a solution-focused approach, we are more likely to ask, "When does success happen already and how can we do more of that?" than "What is happening when it is going wrong and how do we fix that?"

APPRECIATIVE APPROACHES

At about the same time that solution-focused approaches were emerging, David Cooperrider and colleagues at Case Western Reserve University were pioneering the appreciative inquiry approach to organizational change. At its heart, it proposes an *inquiry* into what can be *appreciated* in any organization and then uses these identified strengths as the basis for change. Some key principles emphasized within this appreciative approach include:

Future Images Influence Current Behaviors

Proponents of Appreciative Inquiry (AI) suggest that perceptions of the future have an important influence on the present (Kelm, 2005). In addition, it is proposed that positive images lead to positive futures becoming self-fulfilling prophecies. The GROWTH system leverages this principle with its focus on creating a positive image of the future in the form of a richly articulated, emotionally engaging goal. The more this preferred future can be embellished using the whole range of sensory imagery, the more powerfully it acts as a magnet drawing people toward it.

This focus on the future and its role in shaping the present is given further support in the recently published *Homo Prospectus* (Seligman, Railton, Baumeister, & Sripada, 2016). The authors propose that the ability to think imaginatively about the future may in fact be the *defining* characteristic that distinguishes human beings from other animals. "[W]e believe that the unrivalled human ability to be guided by imagining alternatives stretching into the future—'prospection'—uniquely describes *Homo sapiens*" (Seligman et al., 2016, p. ix).

Words Create Worlds

A key concept within these positive approaches is the way in which language is central to how we make sense of the present and create the future. The words we use shape our experiences, the meaning that we give them, and the way we change them. This concept highlights the fundamental importance of questions in the coaching process. David Cooperrider (2017) argues that "[p]eople live in the worlds our questions create." As coaches, we want our coachees to live in resourceful worlds and to be more intentional about the words used to describe the world they inhabit. It is particularly important that they imagine the positive future world they wish to move toward.

"Through conversations we form and reform our life experiences and events; we create and recreate our meanings and understandings; and we construct and reconstruct our realities and ourselves. Some conversations enhance possibility; others diminish it."

—Jackie Kelm, *Appreciative Living* (2015)

POSITIVE PSYCHOLOGY

Professor Martin Seligman (2002, 2011) launched the term *positive psychology* in 1998, giving a stronger, more explicit focus to the scientific study of human flourishing. He argued that the field of psychology should pay more attention to what makes life worth living rather than merely focusing on human weakness and mental illness. A number of the key concepts of Positive Psychology are discussed below.

The Impact of Positive Emotions

Positive psychologists believe that making change happen and sustaining it requires large amounts of positive energy. Barbara Fredrickson's work (2001) on positive emotions (such as hope, kindness, joy, peace, and gratitude) has advanced thinking in this area through her "broaden and build theory." In essence, Fredrickson's research led her to conclude that certain positive emotions are not simply pleasant feelings but play a role in helping people *broaden* their thinking (by creating more possibilities and expanding their perspective) and *build* more robust emotional resources that develop resilience and overall well-being. This increased resilience helps people bounce back from stresses and disappointments more quickly. This way of understanding positive emotions allows coaches to appreciate the importance of supporting their coachees to experience positive emotions in their daily lives.

The Value of Leveraging Strengths

Various researchers and practitioners have been active in the area of strengths identification and development (Buckingham, 2007; Peterson & Seligman, 2004). Positive psychologists propose that people grow most in the area of their greatest strength, not the opposite, as is commonly assumed. Further, it is argued that identifying strengths and using them more broadly is the most effective way to grow and develop.

IN DEPTH: Values in Action

The Values in Action (VIA) Inventory developed by Peterson and Seligman (2004) provides a research-based resource that explicitly identifies universally recognized strengths. The VIA survey, which helps people identify their signature strengths, can be accessed free of charge from http://www.viacharacter.org/www/Character-Strengths-Survey.

The Importance of Hope

Snyder and Lopez (2005) pioneered work exploring the links between hope and motivation toward achieving goals. Those with high levels of hope demonstrate a range of benefits compared to those with lower levels of hope (Lopez, 2013). It is proposed that a significant influence on levels of hope are *Pathways Thinking* and *Agency Thinking. Pathways Thinking* refers to the ability to generate various routes from the present to the desired future. *Agency Thinking* refers to the level of intention, confidence, and ability to follow various pathways toward the desired future. It is argued that a cyclical relationship exists between Agency Thinking and Pathways Thinking—increasing the sense of agency helps generate more pathways and more options helps increase agency—both contributing to a growing sense of hope (see Figure 5.1).

FIGURE 5.1 Growing Hope

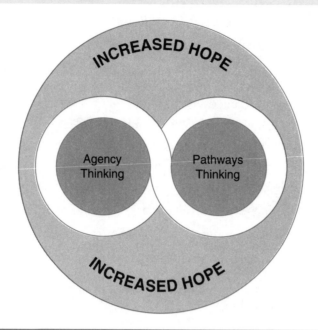

SOURCE: © Growth Coaching International.

SELF-DETERMINATION THEORY

Self-Determination Theory (SDT) has come to the fore over the last 30 years as a seminal theory exploring and explaining the core principles of sustainable human motivation (Ryan & Deci, 2000). In essence, SDT argues that all human beings possess positive tendencies toward growth and development that are enhanced by an environment that supports three innate and universal psychological needs: (1) **autonomy**—having a sense of choice, (2) **competence**—using capabilities to make an impact, and (3) **relatedness**—being in community with others. When these basic needs are met, people operate in an environment that actively nourishes human thriving. This theory demonstrates the significance of coaching in supporting people to be engaged and motivated at work. Coaching places responsibility and choice with the coachee, thereby supporting her to experience autonomy. The process of coaching is designed to support people to use their skills and experiences to make an impact within their contexts. In this way, it helps people feel competent. And, as we have already discussed, coaching relies on a relationship between two individuals. Furthermore, coaching often supports coachees to improve relationships with the people around them. By addressing the three psychological needs of human beings, coaching can have a significant impact on their success and well-being.

HOW CAN WE APPLY THESE POSITIVE THEORIES WHILE USING THE GROWTH FRAMEWORK?

In essence, knowing that these approaches underpin the GROWTH system means that an effective coach supports her coachee to:

- Get clear (in a detailed way) about "what is wanted" instead of an extended conversation about what is not wanted and its causes

- Identify any resources, strengths, and skills that might be useful in moving toward the preferred future

- Acknowledge, affirm, and amplify any identified resources and strengths

- Take small steps toward the described preferred future

- Monitor progress and do more of what is helping

- If it is not helping, change and do something else

There are specific ways in which these perspectives influence the application of the GROWTH model (see Figure 5.2).

Some of these are highlighted in the Coaching Tips on the facing page.

FIGURE 5.2 The GROWTH Model

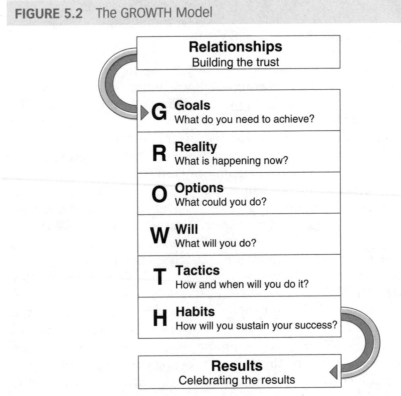

SOURCE: Campbell, J. (2016). Framework for practitioners 2: THE GROWTH model. In C. van Nieuwerburgh (Ed.), *Coaching in professional contexts* (pp. 235–240). London, UK: SAGE. © Growth Coaching International.

COACHING TIPS: Build Trust and Relationship

- During initial interactions, look for things that can be genuinely affirmed and express those through genuine compliments.

- As much as possible, create a safe space that helps the coachee develop positive expectations about the coaching conversation(s):
  - Listen actively
  - Guarantee confidentiality
  - Minimize any power differential

- When reconnecting for a follow-up conversation, begin with a question that focuses on what has been working since the previous session. Ask, "What's been a highlight for you from last time?" or simply, "What's better since the last time we met?" This focus helps get the session started on a positive note.

- Building genuine rapport helps establish "connectedness."

Goal

- When exploring the Goal, encourage your coachee to build a very detailed vision of a preferred future. Ask detail-seeking questions like:
  - What specifically do you want?
  - How will things be better for you when that happens?
  - How will you know when you have achieved it?
  - What specific things would be happening that would tell you that?
  - What would you be hearing others say when you achieve this outcome?
  - Can you paint a picture of what's happening when these changes are in place?

- Specifically explore what it will feel like to achieve the outcomes being considered. The emotional dimension has a significant impact on the level of commitment generated. Ask, "What benefits will you enjoy as a result of achieving this goal?"

- Invite your coachee to choose the area of focus, highlighting her autonomy in the coaching process.

- Help a coachee reframe challenging situations so that other perspectives can enlarge the dimensions of any topic she might be exploring. You can help a coachee reframe situations by helping her consider the issue from a later time perspective ("What will this look like in 5 years?") or from the viewpoint of others ("How would this look through your students' eyes?").

Reality

- In Reality, focus on "what is working already?" Use a 1–10 scale to measure progress toward the preferred future. Sometimes it works best to draw a scale on a page or whiteboard.

  Ask, "If '10' represents the preferred future you just described already happening and '1' represents the worst this situation has ever been, how far along on this scale are you now?" The scale provides an opportunity to affirm progress already made: "Tell me what's already in place that gets you that high on the scale and not lower." The 'R' in GROWTH can therefore stand for *Resources* as well as Reality.

- Look for anything that might be a useful resource and name, affirm, and amplify this. Ask, "How did you manage to do that?"

- Always look for an opportunity to affirm any strengths that might emerge at this stage in the conversation. "I'm impressed by x. From what you just said it seems that you have a strength in x." All this assists in building Agency Thinking and leads to greater hopefulness.

- Focusing on progress so far and the strengths being deployed helps build the sense of competence, increasing motivation.

- Use the simple question "What else?" to explore the current Reality from a resourceful perspective more fully. Ask, "What else gets you that high on the scale?"

COACHING TIPS: The "What Else?" Question

- The respectful use of the short question "What else?" or "And what else?" can be one of the most helpful of coaching questions. When asked in a curious tone, it prompts the coachee to explore the topic beyond what she may have previously considered or have been able to express.

- In using this question it helps if it is *What else?* and not *Anything else?* The former presupposes there *is* something else and this assumption itself tends to gently prompt further exploration.

- It is important to ask the "What else?" question more often than you would in a regular conversation but not so frequently that it irritates the coachee.

- It also helps if a curious tone is maintained. If the "What else?" question is asked in a way that conveys a sense of interrogation it is much less effective, even unhelpful.

Options

- When generating Options, first explore signs of one step higher on the scale. Generate options around how to get to the next step. This keeps the focus on small step progress.

- Try to help your coachee generate several options by using the "What else?" question several times. Generating more options leads to greater levels of Pathways Thinking and greater hopefulness.

- Help make the generation of options light and fun. Positive emotions at this time can lead to a broadening of perspective and greater creativity.

- Again, inviting choice among options highlights autonomy.

Will

- When inviting a choice among options ask, "Which of these options energizes you the most?"

Tactics

- Help your coachee identify small, even tiny, next steps. Ask, "What is the first step you could take to progress this in the next 48 hours?"

Habits

- Encourage your coachee to use her strengths as she progresses her current goals. Ask, "How can you use your strengths here to develop some specific approaches to achieve your goal?"

- Ask your coachee to think more intentionally about her strengths, how she has used these in the past, and how they might help implement the options chosen.

- Help your coachee design her weekly activities so that they are based around her strengths.

Celebrate Results

- Focus on the future and the positive things that the coachee is moving toward, especially any positive emotions that will be experienced when the goal is achieved.

- Intentionally and explicitly celebrate any progress.

And in General . . .

- Throughout the whole GROWTH framework, build a repertoire of positive questions to help your coachee focus on resourceful, progress-focused language.

- Remember to be succinct—too many of your words can reduce the impact of the question or comment.

CONCLUSION

It has been argued that coaching is a form of applied positive psychology since both fields are dedicated to helping people learn and flourish (Leach & Green, 2016; van Nieuwerburgh & Green, 2014). Important to note, positive psychology reminds us of the need to support both the achievement and well-being of our coachees. Coaching, whether formal or informal, provides a context in which many of the concepts and strategies emerging from the field of positive psychology can be applied.

EXPLORE FURTHER

- To learn more about Solution-Focused approaches, read Shennan's *Solution-Focused Practice*.

- To learn more about Appreciative Inquiry, read Hammond's *The Thin Book of Appreciative Inquiry*.

- To learn more about Hope Theory, read Lopez's *Making Hope Happen*.

- To learn more about Self-Determination Theory and Coaching, read Spence and Oades' *Coaching With Self-Determination in Mind*.

- To learn more about developing positive emotions, read Fredrickson's *Positivity*.

- To learn more about Positive Psychology, read Boniwell's *Positive Psychology in a Nutshell*.

SMALL STEP STARTER

Go online and complete the VIA Strengths Survey and identify your five signature strengths at http://www.viacharacter.org/www/Character-Strengths-Survey.

Share these with a trusted colleague or friend; ask them to give examples of how these strengths show up.

And/or reflect on these questions:

- How do I see these strengths playing out in my leadership, in my coaching?

- If I were to use these strengths just a little bit more, what might I notice? What might others notice?

REFERENCES

Boniwell, I. (2012). *Positive psychology in a nutshell: The science of happiness* (3rd ed.). Maidenhead, Berkshire, UK: Open University Press.

Buckingham, M. (2007). *Go put your strengths to work: Six powerful steps to achieve outstanding performance*. New York, NY: Simon & Schuster.

Cameron, K. S., Dutton, J. E., Quinn, R. E., & Editors. (2003). *Positive organizational scholarship: Foundations of a new discipline*. San Francisco, CA: Berrett-Koehler.

Cooperrider, D. (2017). *Appreciative inquiry: Positive core of change*. Presentation delivered at University of St.Thomas, MN. Retrieved from http://slideplayer.com/slide/8334535/

De Shazer, S., Korman, H., Berg, I. K., & Trepper, T. (2007). *More than miracles: The state of the art of solution-focused brief therapy*. New York, NY: Routledge.

Fredrickson, B. (2011). *Positivity: Groundbreaking research to release your inner optimist and thrive*. Richmond, VA: Oneworld.

Fredrickson, B. L. (2001). The role of positive emotions in positive psychology: The broaden-and-build theory of positive emotions. *American Psychologist, 56*(3), 218–226.

Greer, N. (2010). The coaching manager. *InterAction, 2*(2), 28–43.

Hammond, S. A. (1996). *The thin book of appreciative inquiry*. Lima, OH: CSS Publishing Company.

Hefferon, K., & Boniwell, I. (2011). *Positive psychology theory, research and applications*. Maidenhead, Berkshire, UK: McGraw-Hill International.

Iveson, C., George, E., & Ratner, H. (2011). *Brief coaching: A solution focused approach*. London, UK: Routledge.

Jackson, P. Z., & McKergow, M. (2002). *The solutions focus: The SIMPLE way to positive change (people skills for professionals)*. London, UK: Nicholas Brealey International.

Kelm, J. B. (2015). *Appreciative living: The principles of appreciative inquiry in daily life*. Charleston, SC: Venet.

Leach, C., & Green, S. (2016). Integrating coaching and positive psychology in education. In C. van Nieuwerburgh (Ed.), *Coaching in professional contexts*. London, UK: SAGE.

Lopez, S. J. (2013). *Making hope happen: Create the future you want for yourself and others*. New York, NY: Simon & Schuster.

O'Connor, S., & Cavanagh, M. (2013). The coaching ripple effect: The effects of developmental coaching on wellbeing across organizational networks. *Psychology of Well-Being: Theory, Research and Practice, 3*(1), 2.

Peterson, C., & Seligman, M. E. P. (2004). *Character strengths and virtues: A handbook and classification*. Washington, DC: American Psychological Association.

Ryan, R., & Deci, E. (2000). Self-determination theory and the facilitation of intrinsic motivation, social development, and well-being. *American Psychologist, 55*(1), 68–78.

Seligman, M. E. P. (2002). *Authentic happiness: Using the new positive psychology to realize your potential for lasting fulfillment*. New York, NY: Simon & Schuster.

Seligman, M. E. P. (2011). *Flourish: A visionary new understanding of happiness and well-being*. New York, NY: Simon & Schuster.

Seligman, M. E. P., Railton, P., Baumeister, R. F., & Sripada, C. (2016). *Homo prospectus*. New York, NY: Oxford University Press.

Shennan, G. (2014). *Solution-focused practice: Effective communication to facilitate change*. London, UK: Palgrave Macmillan.

Snyder, C., & Lopez, S. (2005). *Handbook of positive psychology*. Oxford, UK: Oxford University Press.

Spence, G., & Oades, L. (2011). Coaching with self-determination in mind: Using theory to advance evidence-based coaching practice. *International Journal of Evidence Based Coaching and Mentoring, 9*(2), 37–55.

van Nieuwerburgh, C., & Green, S. (2014). Developing mental toughness in young people: Coaching as an applied positive psychology. In D. Strycharczyk & P. Clough (Eds.), *Developing mental toughness in young people for the twenty first century*. London, UK: Karnac.

Whitney, D., Trosten-Bloom, A., & Cooperrider, D. (2010). *The power of appreciative inquiry: A practical guide to positive change* (2nd ed.). San Francisco, CA: Berrett-Koehler.

Visit **www.growthcoaching.com.au** for more coaching and professional learning resources for educators.

CHAPTER 6

Using a Coaching Approach to Enhance the Performance and Well-Being of Teachers

Principals and school leaders are responsible for the performance and development of staff in their schools. In their roles, they will typically initiate and support a range of professional learning activities designed to enhance the performance and well-being of staff. Recent research confirms what many educators have known intuitively: that the quality of teaching is central to the learning experience of students (Hattie, 2012). As a result, school resources have been allocated to a range of professional learning activities designed to help teachers continue to improve their pedagogy and teaching practices.

As part of this commitment to enhancing classroom practice, school leaders also manage a range of mechanisms designed to review the professional performance of teachers. For many leaders, in both corporate and educational settings, this is often viewed as a challenging leadership task (Lueger, 2006a). Formal performance review and appraisal processes are sometimes complex and considered problematic. In some cases, they are avoided altogether. In other cases, they can become "check box" exercises, carried out in a perfunctory manner. Often, the exercise does not deliver improved performance and can even result in strained relationships between leaders and members of their team (Lueger, 2006a).

This chapter explores

- Some background on formal performance review processes
- How coaching approaches can bring the best elements of coaching to transform performance review conversations
- The key differences when using a coaching approach in performance review conversations

- Three school system experiences describing differing approaches to using coaching in this context

- Some practical tools that can help integrate a coaching approach into performance review conversations

SOME BACKGROUND ON PERFORMANCE REVIEW PROCESSES

There is little doubt that reviewing the performance of staff in any organization is an important and reasonable component of organizational effectiveness. Knowing what people are achieving (or not achieving) in relation to organizational, team, and individual objectives is a necessary part of management. At the same time, it is important to be aware of how people are performing so that it is possible to support them to continue to contribute in a positive way. Somewhat surprisingly, however, it seems to be the case that performance review conversations are not always experienced positively by team members.

Typical criticisms from the corporate context include

- The performance review process is too bureaucratic

- Feedback is provided so late that it is not possible to make changes

- Rating systems are too subjective

- Forced rankings are unfair

- Performance review processes can damage relationships

- Performance review meetings promise what they cannot deliver (Winter, 2009, p. 9)

Within education, similar concerns have been raised. An OECD (2013) report on education commented:

> [N]early half of all teachers in Australia (43%) report that appraisal and feedback systems in their school have had little or no impact on the way teachers teach in the classroom. The majority (62%) believe that appraisal and feedback is primarily an administrative exercise, and this has a detrimental effect on their job satisfaction. (p. 19)

Educators in other countries have expressed related concerns. In Canada, similar levels of dissatisfaction were revealed in a recent major study that explored teachers' views on performance appraisal (Maharaj, 2014). Furthermore, the Sutton Trust in the UK recognized that there are concerns with the various approaches that are currently used to evaluate teachers' performance (Murphy, 2013).

While in principle, performance reviews serve a useful organizational purpose, in practice they can be problematic. Indeed, it has been reported that several high profile corporate organizations are now replacing their performance review processes (Marr, 2015). What seems to be replacing the existing annual performance review meeting is a system of more regular, more informal feedback check-ins, goal setting, and coaching (Cappelli, 2016; Hassell, 2015).

HOW ADOPTING A COACHING APPROACH CAN BRING THE BEST ELEMENTS OF COACHING TO TRANSFORM PERFORMANCE REVIEW CONVERSATIONS

As we have discussed previously, many of the core elements of effective coaching can transfer easily into a whole range of school leadership contexts—leading teams, managing "on the run" interactions, working with parents and in conversations with students. None of these situations would be recognized as formal coaching, and yet adopting a coaching approach and skillfully deploying many of the elements of coaching can make these conversations more satisfying and productive for both parties. Similarly, we recognize that performance review conversations are not coaching conversations, and yet they too can be much more effective interactions when conducted with a coaching approach.

Elements of Typical Organizational Performance Review Conversations

- Assessing performance

- Setting objectives

- Measuring performance against set criteria

- Input from manager

- Links to reward systems

- Clear power difference between reviewer and reviewee

- Provision of feedback

- Gap analysis

- Initiated by manager

- Recorded and monitored

(Continued)

(Continued)

- Uses predetermined recording templates
- Information is stored
- Compulsory
- Provides support and challenge

Elements of Typical Organizational Coaching Conversations

- Safety
- Setting objectives and goals
- Focus on professional and personal development
- Initiated by the coachee
- Provides support and challenge
- Encouraging climate
- Challenging feedback
- Coach and coachee are equals
- Affirming feedback
- Most input from coachee
- Focus on present and future
- Non-judgmental stance
- Confidential
- Voluntary
- Any written records for learning purposes only and designed and owned by the coachee

What elements of coaching can make a constructive difference to these conversations? The following orientations, skills, and practices can be incorporated into formal performance review conversations:

- Giving greater attention to what future excellent performance might look like

    Ask: "What would you be noticing if performance was excellent in this area? What would others be noticing you doing?"

- Exploring and affirming strengths and how to leverage them for greater success

  Ask: "Based on what you have shared, it seems like you have a strength in x. How might you use that strength in other areas of your role?"

- Recognizing weaker areas of performance and exploring ways to work around them if possible, or getting skills in these areas to "good enough"

  Ask: "What is 'good enough' performance in this area? How might we structure aspects of your role to ensure this is achieved?"

- Focusing on learning, development of self-awareness, and personal responsibility

  Ask: "What can you learn from this experience? What other choices could you make to improve the way this works?"

- Inviting reviewees to help identify goals and targets

  Ask: "As you look at the school's priorities for this year, your own teaching load, and how you want your teaching to be by the end of the year, what would be your high leverage areas for development? What professional standards might be most relevant for your development?"

- Ensuring that goals have a good level of stretch but are not unattainable

  Ask: "What specific measures do we need to include to ensure this goal has challenge and is also reachable?"

- Practicing great listening and thought-provoking questions

  Focus on inviting responses and genuinely listening.

- Setting up more frequent check-in and feedback sessions throughout the year

  Schedule regular check-ins at the beginning of the year. Consider progress, review goals, and establish small steps.

- Adopting more flexible rating and/or scaling approaches

  Use a solution-focused scaling technique (presented later in this chapter)

- Exploring systemic issues that might support goal attainment and minimizing the impact of those that might work against success

  Ask: "How might I support you to achieve these goals? What processes could we modify to support achievement of these goals?"

Small changes in the conversational stance can make a potentially big, positive difference. For example, if a leader is to approach a review conversation from a strengths perspective, an exchange might look like this:

Team member:	"I used to manage my time poorly but I am much better at it now."
Leader:	"Sounds like you have made some real progress in this area. What made you decide to start using your time more productively?"

Such a response does several things:

- It begins with an affirmation that acknowledges progress.

- It focuses on amplifying what is working better.

- It acknowledges the responsibility taken to make improvements.

- It avoids asking "What stopped your poor time management?" This question invites the colleague to explore influences on the change from outside.

- It avoids an exploration of poor time management practices.

As a result of adopting this conversational stance, an entirely different and more useful conversation emerges.

WHAT ARE THE KEY DIFFERENCES BETWEEN PERFORMANCE APPRAISAL AND COACHING CONVERSATIONS?

It is important to re-emphasize that despite using a coaching approach, performance review conversations are not the same as formal coaching conversations. When the evaluative, assessment element is retained in performance review conversations, it changes a fundamental aspect of the interaction. Further, the person leading the performance review process is invariably in a more powerful position within the organization and therefore able to determine career enhancing or career limiting implications from the process. When assessment takes place and hierarchical power is involved, trust is likely to be impacted, safety is jeopardized, new insights may be limited, autonomy may be diminished, and learning and growth are less likely (Stanier, 2016). As a result, these conversations cannot be considered to be formal coaching sessions. All of this is not to say that performance reviews should not happen. What we are proposing is that conversations about performance should be more frequent and will be more effective when leaders adopt a coaching approach.

Even though we advocate integrating good coaching elements into performance review conversations, there is a danger that even using the term *coaching approach* in these situations could potentially confuse those involved and end up undermining other coaching initiatives in the school.

New Zealand

Kerry Mitchell, Director, The Education Group, Auckland, NZ

Teacher appraisal in New Zealand seeks to incorporate both professional growth and accountability streams within the one appraisal system. The professional growth component explores goal setting and inquiry into practice while the accountability component addresses issues related to renewal of a license to teach (practicing certificate). At the heart of this is a commitment to the twin goals of strengthening the culture of self-responsibility as well as accountability and improvement.

There is a strong focus in New Zealand on the alignment between appraisal, inquiry into practice, and professional learning and development. Alignment is achieved through:

- Professional leaders and teachers having a strong understanding about the national criteria for teachers (Practicing Teachers Criteria) and being able to describe what effective practice looks like. The Practicing Teacher Criteria describe what a teacher should know, value, and do as a professional.

- Developing a culture of self-responsibility: This feature represents the greatest mind-set shift for both individuals and organizations to make. The enactment of responsibility to self and others takes both the professional leader and the teacher into an active role in appraisal and professional learning.

- Professional inquiry into practice: This involves teachers setting goals that are based on their own learning needs and the needs of their students.

- Evaluative capability: This process allows teachers to authentically examine their practice and its impact on learners. They can use the information to further strengthen and develop their practice.

- Having a strong coaching culture: Coaching is integral to the process and supports teachers to progress and achieve their goals. By engaging in respectful coaching conversations about professional practice, teachers become better able to test their assumptions and beliefs. Briefly, when they stay open to learning about how they are thinking about or reacting to a situation they are far more likely to genuinely co-construct a solution to a problem or challenge.

- Using the professional inquiry process to curate evidence of practice so that every 3 years teachers are able to demonstrate their competencies and renew their practicing certificate.

(Continued)

(Continued)

Scotland, United Kingdom
Margaret Barr, Former Secondary Head Teacher, Glasgow, Scotland

Within the education system in Scotland the streams of professional growth and accountability are separate. All teachers are entitled and required to engage in Professional Update, which is the approach to professional growth linked to continued registration with the General Teaching Council for Scotland. With Professional Update, the vehicle for continuous improvement is professional learning, not an appraisal or performance management system.

This approach is founded on a professional review and development process, and its features are:

- The process begins with teachers' own self-evaluation of their practice, against the professional standards. Then, in discussion with their line manager or other reviewer, they set professional learning targets relevant to school priorities and their own career aspirations. Throughout the year, teachers keep a reflective record of their professional learning and evidence of its impact on student learning. Discussion is ongoing, with one formal meeting each year.

- Coaching has a key role in Professional Update, and reviewers are required to use coaching and mentoring approaches throughout the process.

- Every 5 years, teachers and reviewers complete the Professional Update sign-off, to confirm that the engagement in professional review has been taking place.

Teachers with a performance weakness should recognize it in their ongoing self-evaluation. Alternatively based on other evidence (e.g., class observations) the line manager will raise the matter of underperformance and will provide a range of supports, which could include coaching. If the performance concerns become significant despite support, a separate competence process begins.

During the competence process, the Professional Update sign-off is postponed, but the teacher is still required to engage with all other elements of Professional Update.

United States
Joellen Killion, Senior Advisor, Learning Forward

In the United States, professional learning and performance evaluation systems have long been distinct silos. Within the last 8 years, policy makers, researchers, and education practitioners have worked to close the gap between the two systems.

Driven by federal incentive programs such as *Race to the Top* and accountability measures, state education leaders redesigned educator performance appraisals systems to integrate more purposeful alignment among educator performance evaluation, professional growth, and student achievement. This alignment mirrored research- and evidence-based practices educators were implementing in schools to elevate student learning in standards-based curriculum and instruction, ongoing formative assessment, and data-driven instruction. Between 2010 and 2015, in response to such incentives and regulations, 43 states added measures of student achievement as evidence of teacher effectiveness to their educator evaluation and support programs.

In late 2015, the pendulum swung yet again with the passage of the *Every Student Succeeds Act* (ESSA). This latest revision of the *Elementary and Secondary Education Act* increased states' flexibility, limited federal involvement in education, and *removed* the requirement for measures of student achievement from evaluation and support systems. The new act requires multiple measures of educator performance, high-quality evaluation tools, training for supervisors on differentiating performance, constructive feedback, and use of data to inform decisions regarding professional learning, improvement systems, and personnel decisions, and ongoing auditing of evaluation and development systems. ESSA opened the door for states to once again revise educator evaluation and support systems; many are already at work changing their systems. The new Act also defines research-based attributes required for professional learning funded through federal programs that encompass developing educator capacity. While states launch this new body of work to revamp their educator evaluation and support systems, the 2016 election has given rise to a new federal effort to remove even these basic federal requirements and leave all decisions regarding education to states.

Although states have considerable time to respond to the new regulations, the predominant direction of states getting an early start on revising their evaluation and support systems is likely to emphasize educator growth and support over evaluation. While integrating the systems is surely warranted, the capacity at the systems and talent levels to operationalize such integration is currently, and may continue to be, challenging. Supervisors with the desire to support growth through professional learning and constructive feedback are often ill-prepared to provide educators with the intensive, continuous, and focused support needed to sustain change in practice and accentuate continuous improvement over evaluation. The training supervisors received for their current evaluation systems emphasized accuracy in measurement and judgment rather than the creation of systems for professional growth. Traditional professional learning and growth systems across the United States are insufficiently comprehensive and remain, in many cases,

(Continued)

(Continued)

disconnected from the everyday work of educators. Other systems, such as those for strategic improvement, personnel performance evaluation, student assessment, and human capital, lack sufficient coherence and alignment with professional learning and growth systems. Yet evidence is emerging in districts where these systems align that students are benefiting.

One indicator that professional learning more closely aligns with performance evaluation is replacing time requirements for engagement with results measured by increases in educator practice and student achievement. The number of hours spent on professional learning continues to be a predominant measure. Expectations for results are integrated into current evaluation system rather than in professional learning, yet with the relaxed federal guidelines about including student achievement measures in performance evaluation, states will no longer be required to align their systems.

Another indicator of closer alignment is embedding professional learning within the daily practice of educators so that it emphasizes educator practice and student results. Some states, districts, and schools are rearranging school day schedules to provide time for collaborative learning and work as routine within the work day rather than occasional professional development days scattered throughout a school year. Others are implementing coaching programs for principals and teachers to personalize, sustain, intensify, and embed professional growth; however, the implementation of coaching can be challenging. The ratio of coaches to educators remains too uneven to ensure that every educator receives sufficient amounts of coaching for continuous professional growth. While investments in coaching provide more professional learning and constructive feedback for educators, the effects are mixed because it is inadequately implemented. Increased time for professional learning within school days, another frequent structural change in U.S. schools, is also not producing sufficient results, largely because there is a high degree of variance in quality of and access to relevant opportunities for professional growth. Other changes in ESSA reduce allowable expenditures for professional learning, which may in turn decrease educators' opportunity to strengthen their professional practice.

The newly legislated changes, designed to increase states' flexibility and accountability for educator evaluation and professional growth, may disappear altogether if promised elimination of federal oversight or involvement in education occurs. With states being responsible now for both educator quality and professional growth, variance across states in educator preparation, performance, and professional learning is likely to grow across the United States.

SOME PRACTICAL TOOLS AND PROCESSES THAT CAN HELP INTEGRATE A POSITIVE, COACHING APPROACH INTO PERFORMANCE REVIEW CONVERSATIONS

Beginnings and Endings

How things start and how things end are important. A poor beginning to any performance review conversation makes it very difficult to make up lost ground and ensure a positive outcome. What things can you do to help any performance review conversation begin well?

- Get the physical environment right—including room set up that minimizes the power differential.

- Show that you are prepared for the meeting.

- Demonstrate your commitment to the process by allocating sufficient time for the conversation.

- Clarify expectations about the desired outcomes and agree at the outset how the conversation will proceed.

- Start with a question that invites a positive response: "In reflecting on the last 6 months at work, what are you most proud of?"

- When concluding, it can be helpful to

  - Clarify what has been agreed regarding future goals and commitments
  - Confirm follow up arrangements and details about how check-ins and progress conversations will take place
  - Confirm any agreed immediate next steps

Encourage Self-Selected Goals Within the Broader School Improvement Framework

Building in an element of choice, even within some broader parameters, preserves a degree of autonomy and reinforces the person's ownership and responsibility within the process. This means that it is helpful to allow the reviewee to select some of her own goals, ensuring that these align with the strategic objectives of the school.

Encourage Small Step Movement

Consistent with a solution-focused approach is an increasing emphasis on making small step commitments toward goals supported by more frequent formal and informal check-ins on progress. It is important that the review process is understood as taking place across the entire year, not in one extended meeting.

Work Toward Building a Culture of Receiving Feedback

A recently published book, *Thanks for the Feedback* (Stone & Heen, 2014), highlights the importance of learning how to discern and respond to feedback. This is a relatively overlooked skill that is critical to the way that feedback is acted on. (See Chapter 7 for more specific suggestions about how to do this.)

Consider the 100 Point Scale as an Alternative Way of Discussing Past Performance

In recent years, approaches to discussing performance based on appreciative inquiry and a solution-focused approach have emerged. These theoretical perspectives are aligned with the values and practices of coaching. One particular approach to scaling and rating achievements and performance is the Solution-Focused Rating Scale (Lueger, 2006a). In developing this alternative way of rating performance, Lueger argued the frequently used standard rating scales were based on the following assumptions:

- Performance is static over time.

- Performance is less likely to change and develop.

- The highest rating is the ultimate goal. This therefore tends to focus on the gap between current and ideal performance—in other words, the deficit.

In response, Lueger proposed a more flexible way of reflecting on and rating performance based on distributing 100 points across four levels of performance.

The following outline suggests a way of using this approach within a review conversation:

> "Rate your performance in your current work role since the beginning of the year using the four point scale, allocating 100 points across the 4 categories. Poor; OK; Good; Excellent."

Scale:

Poor————————OK————————Good————————Excellent

10	10	30	50

In this case, the reviewee has indicated that 50% of her work since the beginning of the year has been at Excellent level, 30% of her work has been at Good level, 10% of her work has been at OK level, and 10% at Poor level.

In exploring the Excellent level, ask these kinds of questions:

- When was this?
- What made it excellent?
- What strengths were in play when it was excellent?
- What else?
- How did you do that?
- What would tell you the percentage of excellent is increasing?
- How could this category be made even bigger over the next few months?

The reviewer would then repeat this conversation for any other categories that were identified (i.e., Good, OK, or Poor).

Some further points:

- The information generated from such a conversation forms the basis for setting goals for the future.
- The words used to define levels of performance (Excellent, Good, OK, Poor) can be customized to fit terms used in different school contexts.
- Conversation about performance begins at the positive achievement end of the scale.
- Discussion of anything less than OK performance takes place in the context of a broader conversation that has already recognized strengths and successes (adapted from Lueger, 2006b, pp. 203–209).

LISTEN WITH EARS

This listening and responding framework uses the EARS acronym to prompt a helpful approach to exploring team member reflections in any interaction but it can be particularly helpful in a performance review conversation.

E stands for **Elicit** and involves drawing out success experiences.

Ask questions such as, "What's already working? What's better since last time?"

A is for **Amplify,** which involves expanding and appreciating whatever is working well. This is an attempt to leverage the success experience further and expand it in positive and resourceful directions.

Ask questions such as, "How did you do that?" "How did you know to respond in that way?" "Great. Could you say more about what happened exactly?" "Who else was involved and what do you think they might have noticed?"

The **R** step provides a reminder to **Reinforce** and affirm whatever strength or resource may have been used to achieve the progress.

Share your observations: "To do that must have taken quite a bit of (strength/quality)." "I'm impressed by how you demonstrated x to get to that point."

S stands for **Start** over. This step reminds us to keep searching for more stories and examples of skills, qualities, and personal resources. The more of these that we can help our reviewee articulate and expand on, the more her journey toward the goal begins to look increasingly possible (adapted from Jackson & McKergow, 2006).

CONCLUSION

Leaders who use a coaching approach and demonstrate their care about professional growth and development can bring a positive, constructive emphasis to formal review processes. They welcome these conversations as opportunities to help others learn and move forward. They listen more than they speak. They amplify and leverage strengths. Most important, they encourage realistic self-assessment and the ability to receive feedback well so that successes are celebrated and concerns are tackled in productive and helpful ways.

EXPLORE FURTHER

- To learn more about solution-focused performance review, read Lueger's "Solution-Focused Management—Towards a Theory of Positive Difference."

- To learn more about teacher evaluation practices, read Stiggins' *Defensible Teacher Evaluation*.

- To learn more about evaluative conversations that are also growth-producing and humane, read Abrams' *Hard Conversations Unpacked*.

SMALL STEP STARTER

To begin the process of rethinking (alone or with others) the performance review process in your context, use the 100 Point Scale to get started:

- How much of our current performance review process is:

  Excellent? Good? OK? Poor?

Identify specific examples that support the ratings.

Invite comments in response to these questions:

- What would be happening if there were more excellent practices occurring in our performance review process?
- Which of these additional excellent practices might we be able to introduce in the next 12 months?
- What is our first step toward this?

REFERENCES

Abrams, J. (2016). *Hard conversations unpacked: The whos, the whens, and the what-ifs.* Thousand Oaks, CA: Corwin.

Cappelli, P. (2016). *The annual review revolution.* Retrieved from https://hbr.org/webinar/2016/09/the-annual-review-revolution

Hassell, D. (2015). *How to rethink the Annual Performance Review.* Retrieved from http://www.forbes.com/sites/theyec/2015/12/29/how-to-rethink-the-annual-performance-review/#4d5a57ba7f37

Hattie, J. (2012). *Visible learning for teachers.* London, UK: Routledge.

Jackson, P. Z., & McKergow, M. (2002). *The solutions focus: The SIMPLE way to positive change (people skills for professionals).* London, UK: Nicholas Brealey International.

Lueger, G. (2006a). Solution-focused management—Towards a theory of positive difference. In G. Lueger & X. Korn (Eds.), *Solution-focused management.* Munich, Germany: Rainer Hampp.

Lueger, G. (2006b). Solution-focused rating: New ways in performance appraisal. In G. Lueger & X. Korn (Eds.), *Solution-focused management.* Munich, Germany: Rainer Hampp.

Maharaj, S. (2014). Administrator's views on teacher evaluation: Examining Ontario's teacher performance appraisal. *Canadian Journal of Education Administration and Policy, 152.*

Marr, B. (2015). *How Accenture and Deloitte got rid of performance reviews—And you can too.* Retrieved from http://www.linkedin.com/pulse/how-accenture-deloitte-got-rid-performance-reviews-you-bernard-marr?trk=pulse-det-nav_art

Murphy, R. (2013). *Testing teachers: What works best for teacher evaluation and appraisal.* Retrieved from http://www.suttontrust.com/wp-content/uploads/2013/03/MURPHYTEACHEREVALUATION-FINAL.pdf

OECD. (2013). *The Teaching and Learning International Survey (TALIS) Australia Country Note.* Retrieved from http://www.oecd.org/australia/TALIS-2013-country-note-Australia.pdf

Stanier, M. B. (2016). *The coaching habit: Say less, ask more, and change the way you lead forever.* Toronto, Ontario, Canada: Box of Crayons Press.

Stiggins, R. (2014). *Defensible teacher evaluation: Student growth through classroom assessment.* Thousand Oaks, CA: Corwin.

Stone, D., & Heen, S. (2014). *Thanks for the feedback: The science and art of receiving feedback well.* New York, NY: Penguin.

Winter, G. (2009). *The man who cured the performance review: A practical and engaging guide to perfecting the art of performance conversation.* Sydney, Australia: John Wiley & Sons.

Visit **www.growthcoaching.com.au** for more coaching and professional learning resources for educators.

CHAPTER 7

Creating the Right Context for Feedback

In this chapter, the importance of feedback as a component part of leadership conversations is explored. Teachers have long been committed to the value of providing feedback in the context of student learning and in recent times the significance of this has been emphasized even more (Hattie & Timperley, 2007). It is now widely accepted that feedback is vital to adult and professional learning.

It has been proposed that giving feedback is one of the most helpful ways in which a school leader can live out her leadership role (Grissom, Loeb, & Master, 2013). We have also argued in this book that giving feedback is one of the key coaching skills. Further, we propose that leaders can take a role in helping people discern the value of feedback and respond to it in constructive ways. In fact, learning how to *receive* feedback positively is as important as the ability to provide feedback.

SCHOOL LEADER AS "CONVERSATIONAL LEADER"

If we accept the view that schools are networks of people engaged in various forms of conversation designed to progress the purpose and goals of the school (Campbell, 2016), then the leader is a key person in setting the conversational tone. This view of schools requires the leader to be aware of, and to intentionally influence, the content and style of every interaction. Feedback conversations are important leadership conversations.

In addition, giving feedback is one of the core skills in the GROWTH Coaching System and the ability to give and receive feedback is an important leadership skill. It has been argued that both giving *and receiving* feedback are important factors when creating an environment for growing and learning (van Nieuwerburgh, 2017). We would argue that it is central to establishing an effective leadership coaching approach. One recent study (Grissom et al., 2013) has proposed that providing feedback was the most significant way in which leaders could make the biggest impact on teaching practice.

Typically, the term *feedback* carries some negative connotations and is, for many people, code for *criticism*. Indeed, it could be argued that a school leader has an important role to play in helping establish positive attitudes, knowledge, and skills related to giving and receiving feedback so that this negative perception is diminished. Negative attitudes to feedback may have developed over a period of time so it requires active and sustained effort from leaders. Further, openness to feedback is a key component of a coaching culture (see Chapter 9 for further discussion on this topic).

WHAT IS FEEDBACK?

At its essence, feedback is information that provides an additional perspective about a topic or situation. This additional perspective may reinforce and strengthen current practice or it might invite a change. In the context of coaching, feedback can give a person an alternative perspective that increases her self-awareness or understanding of a situation. According to Stone and Heen (2014), "Feedback includes any information you get about yourself. In the broadest sense, it's how we learn about ourselves from our experiences and from other people—how we learn from life" (p. 4). When described in this way, it would seem that feedback should be welcomed as a way to grow and learn. However, this is not always the case and some of the reasons for this can be found in the way that feedback is given and received.

TYPES OF FEEDBACK

It would seem that feedback serves a purpose in *reinforcing* a way of thinking and acting or invites a *modification* of a way of thinking and acting. In this sense, one type of feedback is *affirming*, in that it indicates support for a current practice and explicitly or implicitly suggests that more of the identified behavior or thinking would be welcomed. Typically, *affirming*, or positive feedback, is considered easier to give and receive. It does seem, however, that some people can have difficulty receiving positive feedback and will seek to discount it, undermining its value. Further, since it seems easier to give, *affirming* feedback is frequently offered in ways that underplay the positive impact that it might have on the receiver.

In contrast, *modifying* feedback invites (or even demands, when safety or legal compliance issues might be at stake) an *alternative* way of thinking and acting. It is *modifying* feedback that has most often been viewed as challenging to give as well as to receive. Since *modifying* feedback, by definition, is inviting change in thinking and acting, this is not surprising.

CONTEXT OF FEEDBACK

This general negative response to feedback is often influenced by the context in which it takes place. The giving of feedback in a formal performance management situation is likely to evoke at least some defensive responses. Of course, this will depend on context, including the quality of the relationship between those involved. Feedback that emerges in a development or learning situation is likely to be received less defensively. As in many situations, the quality of the relationship is an important contextual influence on how feedback is given and received.

TWO SIDES OF FEEDBACK: GIVING AND RECEIVING

In the light of the perceived discomfort of giving feedback, a considerable amount of material has been developed to address the way in which *modifying* feedback is delivered to raise the chances of it being received well (Ontario Principals' Council, 2011). Most of this is helpful, providing theoretical and practical tips and suggestions for leaders engaging in feedback conversations. Much of it is also particularly relevant for coaching conversations.

Less attention has been devoted to exploring various aspects of how people *receive* feedback. A recent publication (Stone & Heen, 2014) has attempted to address this deficit. In the process, the authors make an important point about the relationship between those giving and those receiving feedback. "It doesn't matter how much authority or power a feedback giver has; the receivers are in control of what they do and don't let in, how they make sense of what they're hearing, and whether they choose to change" (Stone & Heen, 2014, p. 9). Given the importance of the receiving side of the feedback relationship, it is helpful to explore how school leaders can contribute to positive and helpful approaches to feedback, both *affirming* and *modifying*, from both the giving and receiving perspectives. Several key aspects of feedback delivery can help ensure that feedback is offered in effective ways.

Language Is Important

Words make a difference. This is a vitally important point, especially in the emotionally charged context of challenging feedback conversations. Considering the words and language patterns to be used or avoided can play an important part in helping others receive feedback well. For example, various feedback structures that intentionally frame words in particular ways have been proposed over recent years. One that has been particularly well received is the Feedback Bridge, which structures the feedback in the following way:

Positive comment(s) . . .

And it would be even better if . . .

Because . . .

How do you see it? (Adapted from Grant & Greene, 2005)

IN CONTEXT: Offering Feedback

Offering feedback using this framework could look like this:

"Your work with your team on a one-to-one basis is excellent. You build a strong connection with each person, you meet with them regularly, and there appears to be high levels of mutual respect.

"And I believe the team would function at an even higher level if your team meetings were better able to leverage the collective thinking of the group because this would mean that the broad experience and knowledge within the team was harnessed for the benefit of everyone.

"How do you see it?"

There are some further points to consider in using this framework:

- Any positive comment at the start *must* be authentic, specific and connected to the following point.

- The *and* is an important word. It is vital that it is not *but*, *although*, or *however*.

- The "because . . ." phrase introduces *why* this is important, something that contributes significantly to gaining buy in.

- The "How do you see it?" question asked after the clear, succinct initial comment conveys the message that there is another point of view to be explored. It recognizes that the feedback provider might not have the whole picture. Finally, it suggests that the feedback provider is curious about the feedback recipient's perspective.

This language scaffold is most often useful when giving challenging feedback, but what about giving *affirming* or positive feedback? Sometimes, leaders are less cautious about the way in which positive feedback is offered. This might be because it is considered easy to deliver. However, some people find it difficult to receive positive feedback, finding ways to discount it, thereby undermining its value and impact.

Some useful principles for giving *affirming* feedback that have an impact:

- Ensuring positive feedback is detailed, specific, and related to observable events

- Providing a specific indication about what *impact* the positive action had on you

- Ensuring that positive feedback is not a generalized comment about the person's character or who they are (Kegan & Lahey, 2001). For example, a comment such as "You're such a kind person" based on one observable act, though well intentioned, can be dismissed by the receiver since they will be aware of many other occasions when they were not kind. The value of this positive comment can therefore be significantly undermined. It is much more powerful if any comment about kindness is merely stated as an observation describing how it impacted you and the specific context in which it occurred.

- Consider whether the feedback recipient would prefer to receive the feedback in writing or in person.

- Consider whether the feedback recipient would prefer to receive the feedback in private or in public.

> "Work settings are language communities . . . all leaders are leading language communities. Though every person, in every setting, has some opportunity to influence the nature of the language, leaders have exponentially greater access and opportunity to shape, alter or ratify the existing language rules."
>
> —Robert Kegan and Lisa Laskow Lahey, *How the Way We Talk Can Change the Way We Work* (2001, p. 8)

Part of a leader's role in helping feedback work well involves building understanding and knowledge about the importance of effective feedback within the school community. The principles described below can help broaden understanding about ways to make feedback work well.

Linking With Goal Setting

At various times, giving challenging feedback has been positioned as a courageous act, acknowledging that giving attention to a topic charged with emotion and potential tension can threaten a good relationship. Raising the issue and getting it out there can indeed take some courage, but sometimes just broaching the topic can be viewed as an end in itself. Offering feedback merely provides an opportunity to work through an issue. However, for a feedback conversation to be useful it must lead to a different, more constructive place. Locke (1996) has made an important point in relation to feedback: "Feedback is most effective in motivating improved performance when it is used to set goals. Feedback alone is just information" (p. 121). Feedback given in the context of coaching conversations is more likely to lead to goal setting. At the same time, it is important to acknowledge that for feedback conversations in any context to be useful, the feedback should lead to movement toward new ways of thinking and acting. Feedback without goal setting, without a conversation about what might be an alternative way of thinking and behaving, is just information. Feedback is less helpful, even damaging, if it is just an exercise in getting something off one's chest.

Affirming feedback can also be an invitation to work toward new goals. Acknowledging a strength can provide an opportunity to encourage the feedback recipient to consider how that strength could be applied more broadly. *Affirming* feedback can be an invitation to stretch and grow, not merely a compliment that generates positive emotions. Some thinkers believe that such feedback is more likely to lead to sustained growth and development than any other kind of feedback (Buckingham, 2007; Buckingham & Clifton, 2001).

New goals can only be explored once the ownership and importance of feedback have been clarified. Does the person receiving feedback *own* it and take *responsibility* for the thinking or behavior that is being given focus? Linked with this sense of taking responsibility is the importance of the topic being raised. Does the person recognize the *importance* of the topic being raised?

The responsibility and importance dimensions are significant in relation to making progress on the topic being explored. Offering feedback involves enlarging a person's awareness in relation to a particular behavior that might need to be modified or which is being affirmed. Until the person receiving feedback (either *affirming* or *modifying*) has owned the feedback and recognized its importance, the feedback is likely to be ignored or lead to resigned compliance (see Figure 7.1).

In any conversation where feedback has been introduced, getting to "Yes, this is important" and "Yes, I take responsibility for this issue" will be necessary for moving forward. In some cases, this may require some time and reflection. However, until ownership and importance are acknowledged, it may prove difficult to start working on the new thinking and behavior required.

FIGURE 7.1 Responsibility, Importance, and Goal Setting

Goal setting begins

Yes, I can take **responsibility.**

YES

Yes, this is **important.**

YES

Focus on decisions coachee may have made that led to the situation.

Give examples. Explain the impact on you and others.

Future Focused

Similarly, feedback that is future focused tends to provide a better chance of being received well. While it might be necessary to explore a particular past situation that may have led to the feedback conversation, it is generally more helpful to spend time on how an alternative way of behaving might look, the benefits that might follow, and the particular strategies that might be useful to pursue. Feedback that is future focused gives attention to things that can be influenced and is more energizing because of that. Excessive time given to talking through a problem or undesirable behavior is not helpful. Instead, the focus should be on what is wanted instead.

Best Interests

Perhaps above all, these tips and strategies for giving effective feedback are less about "what you do" and more about "who you bring" to any feedback interaction. It becomes important to approach any feedback conversation with a level of humility and curiosity. If you can demonstrate that you have the best interests of the other person as a priority, this will increase the possibility of an effective feedback conversation. In such a situation, both parties are likely to feel respected, new behaviors may be explored, and the relationship is strengthened. An exploration of the Coaching Way of Being (van Nieuwerburgh, 2017) is worth considering in these situations.

LEADING THE GIVING OF FEEDBACK

How does the leader in a school positively influence helpful practices in relation to giving feedback? In short, a number of practical principles and concepts can make a positive difference. A leader can assist in the development of a helpful feedback approach by playing a role as a model, educator, and encourager. As a model, it is important that a leader provides clear and consistent role modeling in both giving and receiving feedback. This can involve simply inviting feedback, for example, about a staff meeting and then responding in helpful ways. It might involve giving positive feedback in public after getting permission from the person concerned. Seeing and hearing how feedback can be offered is a very helpful part of learning how to do it. Leaders may also need to educate team members about the importance of feedback, referring to resource materials and studies as a way to build commitment to the value of feedback. As always, getting the balance right is an ongoing challenge.

It is hard to overstate the importance of providing a good role model for how to deliver feedback. Experiencing and observing feedback delivered respectfully, clearly, and effectively sends powerful messages about how to do this well.

LEADING THE RECEIVING OF FEEDBACK

How does the leader in a school positively influence helpful practices in relation to *receiving* feedback? This is an important question given that the power lies with the feedback receiver. The short answer is that the same three roles influencing the effective giving of feedback also contribute to the way in which feedback is received well. Leaders have an opportunity to model, educate, and encourage others in the way that feedback is received, processed, and acted on. As previously indicated, this dimension of feedback has received less attention and yet the way feedback is received is critical for what happens next.

Leaders can take a role in making explicit the way feedback is received. There are occasions when feedback might seem to be well received, but in private the feedback is ignored or resented. There are other occasions when feedback is taken on board too much, too seriously, and too broadly where the person receiving feedback has responded in a way that is disproportionate to the feedback that has been provided.

Stone and Heen (2014) have provided useful insights on this much overlooked dimension of feedback conversations. Some things that are helpful for leaders to consider include:

Developing a "Pull" Feedback Culture

Leaders can play a role that encourages the seeking of feedback and welcoming it as an opportunity to learn and grow. Working toward a belief that every experience—whether regarded as a failure or success—provides an opportunity to learn is a long-term project. However, it is a rewarding project because when that attitude is adopted, perceptions of feedback change significantly.

As part of the journey toward creating a "pull" feedback culture, it can be helpful to make the preferred future in this area a specific intention. Inviting staff to describe what a feedback culture might look like (providing detailed signs of what would be different if a feedback culture were in place) can be very powerful. Involving staff in this kind of explicit conversation about feedback, why it can be vitally important, and how to make it work best can be an important way to bring whole staff awareness and commitment to this way of working. People are less likely to undermine initiatives they have helped create. One thing that could emerge from such a conversation is some clear guidelines related to giving and receiving feedback.

IN CONTEXT: Defining a Feedback Environment

Some questions to explore the establishment of a helpful feedback environment:

- What will we notice about ourselves and others when we have succeeded in establishing an environment where feedback is central to how we work and is helping us all grow and learn?

- What would be the benefits of creating this kind of feedback environment?

- What guidelines might be helpful to establish and agree to in order to maximize the benefits?

Develop Explicit Guidelines for Processing Feedback

Helpful guidelines for processing feedback in constructive ways could include the following suggestions (adapted from Stone & Heen, 2014)

- Making it OK to be able to *choose a time for feedback conversations*: When receiving challenging feedback it is OK for the person receiving feedback to be able to choose the best time for the feedback conversation. For example, "Actually now is not a good time to talk about this. Can we schedule a time later in the week?"

- Focus on *one thing*: It is not uncommon for feedback conversations to spread across a range of topics. When considering a response, it helps if the feedback receiver can narrow the focus to just one area. This is a good principle for feedback providers as well. Giving attention to just one thing raises the chances of the feedback being processed in ways that lead to new thinking and behaviors.

- Encourage an *experimental approach*: Changing a way of thinking or acting rarely occurs with just one step. It is usually more complex than becoming aware of unhelpful patterns or actions and then deciding to do things differently. It will often involve some small step experimentation with different ways of doing things so that trying and not getting it totally right straight away is to be expected. Experimentation and learning from mistakes is to be encouraged.

- Encourage people to *separate the What from the Who*: Issues of identity, of who we are, are often at stake in feedback conversations. If someone highlights something a teacher is not doing so well, it can be easy for her to conclude that she is not an OK teacher or even not an OK person. Negative feedback can send some people into an overreaction that can bring into question their whole identity. It seems that this may be a significant issue for educators given that many teachers view their work as more of a vocation than just a job. Identity as a teacher is central to a person's sense of self so any suggestion of not getting this right can be very threatening.

Raising awareness of this strong identity link will be important. It will therefore be helpful to encourage feedback recipients (and providers) to bring this awareness to their conversations. Model it by inviting feedback and responding to it constructively.

Watch It in Practice

Giving Feedback Using a Coaching Approach

In this chapter, we have highlighted the importance of feedback. Watch this video of a leader adopting a coaching approach when providing feedback.

resources.corwin.com/campbellcoaching

CONCLUSION

In helping build confident, skilled approaches to receiving feedback, there is nothing more powerful than modeling how to do this. If you, as a leader, are prepared to seek feedback and demonstrate how to receive and respond to it well, you will win respect for "walking the talk." Additionally, you begin to create the climate for seeking, giving, and receiving feedback. Moreover, if the leadership team can learn to do this well, further benefits can flow.

While it is acknowledged that providing and receiving feedback can be challenging, it is an important skill. Becoming skilled at the use of feedback and helping others in your team become skilled at this could be one of the most significant school leadership tasks. Since coaching is about learning, conversations that help open up growth opportunities in constructive ways will support the development of empowered school leaders, better teachers, and successful students.

EXPLORE FURTHER

- To learn more about receiving feedback, read Stone and Heen's *Thanks for the Feedback: The Science and Art of Receiving Feedback Well*.

- To learn more about future-focused feedback, read Goldsmith's *Try Feed Forward Instead of Feedback*.

- To learn more about school leaders' feedback, read Grissom, Loeb, and Master's "Effective Instructional Time Use for School Leaders."

- To learn more about feedback in professional learning, read Clark and Duggins' *Using Quality Feedback to Guide Professional Learning: A Framework for Instructional Leaders*.

SMALL STEP STARTER

Make a commitment to start inviting feedback in various interactions in which you are involved. This is certainly not only helpful and easy to do in coaching interactions but also in other conversations and meetings where appropriate.

Preface the asking of the questions by outlining that you are wanting to explore some ways in which you and the organization might get better at giving and receiving feedback.

These simple questions take very little time but can be enormously helpful:

- What's been most useful to you about what we just discussed?

- What was the most helpful thing I did here?

- If we were to meet again to discuss this, is there anything you would like me to do more of or less of next time?

REFERENCES

Buckingham, M. (2007). *Go put your strengths to work: Six powerful steps to achieve outstanding performance*. New York, NY: Simon & Schuster.

Buckingham, M., & Clifton, D. O. (2001). *Now, discover your strengths*. New York, NY: Simon & Schuster.

Campbell, J. (2016). Coaching in schools. In C. J. van Niewerburgh (Ed.), *Coaching in professional contexts*. London, UK: SAGE.

Clark, S., & Duggins, A. (2016). *Using quality feedback to guide professional learning: A framework for instructional leaders*. Thousand Oaks, CA: Corwin.

Goldsmith, M.(2015). *Try feed forward instead of feedback*. Retrieved from http://www.marshallgoldsmith.com/articles/try-feedforward-instead-feedback

Grant, A., & Greene, J. (2005). *Coach yourself at work: Become your own best asset in the workplace*. Sydney, Australia: ABC Books.

Grissom, J. A., Loeb, S., & Master, B. (2013). Effective instructional time use for school leaders: Longitudinal evidence from observations of principals. *Educational Researcher, 42*(8), 433–444.

Hattie, J., & Timperley, H. (2007). The power of feedback. *Review of Educational Research, 77*(1), 81–112. Retrieved from http://dx.doi.org/10.3102/003465430298487

Kegan, R., & Lahey, L. L. (2001). *How the way we talk can change the way we work: Seven languages for transformation*. San Francisco, CA: Jossey-Bass.

Locke, E. A. (1996). Motivation through conscious goal setting. *Applied and Preventive Psychology, 5*(2), 117–124.

Ontario Principals' Council. (2011). *The principal as leader of challenging conversations*. Thousand Oaks, CA: Corwin.

Stone, D., & Heen, S. (2014). *Thanks for the feedback: The science and art of receiving feedback well*. Boston, MA: Harvard Business Review Press.

van Nieuwerburgh, C. (2017). *An introduction to coaching skills: A practical guide* (2nd ed.). London, UK: SAGE.

Visit **www.growthcoaching.com.au** for more coaching and professional learning resources for educators.

CHAPTER 8

Using Coaching Approaches to Enhance the Performance and Well-Being of Teams

In their endeavor to deliver high-quality learning environments, school leaders often work one-to-one with people in the school community. This book has given focus to those one-to-one interactions. Leaders also spend time working with *groups* and *teams* of staff, parents, students, and community groups. Is it possible for a school leader to coach a team in the way we have been exploring in this book? If so, how can school leaders coach a leadership team of which they are an important member?

This chapter explores these questions by considering:

- What is team coaching, and how is it different from individual coaching?

- What are the differences between coaching *groups* and coaching *teams*?

- What are some of the important roles team leaders can play when using a coaching approach with teams?

- How can leaders use the 5Ps framework for team effectiveness?

- How can the coaching approach be used most effectively with teams?

WHAT IS TEAM COACHING, AND HOW IS IT DIFFERENT TO INDIVIDUAL COACHING?

As we have already discussed in this book, we view formal coaching to be a conversation that relies on a powerful, confidential relationship between two people. If this is the case, we cannot talk about a leader undertaking formal coaching with a team or group. We are not saying that it is not possible for teams to experience learning and development through an increase of collective awareness and a sense of team responsibility. Clearly, leaders can deploy coaching skills when working with groups and teams. For example, it is likely that open questions, active listening, and supportive challenge will be welcomed by teams. However, for the sake of definitional clarity, it is important to recognize that the nature and experience of one-to-one coaching conversations and coaching-style group interactions are *essentially* different.

We therefore propose that leaders can employ a *coaching approach* when working with teams and groups. Leaders do this when they support and challenge teams to enhance their effectiveness in achieving their purpose and goals while maintaining themselves in good working order. This coaching approach to working with teams uses many of the key elements of coaching already covered in this book:

- Helping clarify outcomes

- Identifying and exploring resources that can assist in progressing toward desired outcomes

- Exploring options and strategies to help move toward what is wanted

- Incorporating an element of accountability

- Uncovering patterns that help or hinder performance

- Providing insight and clarity through effective listening and questioning

- Agreeing to meet regularly to address certain topics

In summary, leaders can work with teams using a coaching approach by helping teams think well, relate well, and learn well to ensure ongoing team success and well-being.

The most significant difference between formal coaching and the use of coaching approaches with teams is the number of voices in the conversation. In one-to-one coaching, there are two voices—each of equal value. In team contexts, there are multiple voices. The larger the team, the more complex this dynamic becomes.

One aspect that adds to the complexity is the issue of safety. It can be difficult enough to create positive, safe environments even in one-to-one conversations. When working with larger groups of people, this becomes exponentially more difficult. The potential for mistrust and miscommunication increases. Therefore, a key task for a leader using a coaching approach is to nurture an environment that respects differences and encourages openness and trust. Indeed, team development specialist Patrick Lencioni (2002) highlights "lack of trust" as one of the most fundamental team dysfunctions.

While multiple-voice conversations with many perspectives may be more difficult to manage and bring to a successful endpoint, the very richness of perspectives can also bring great potential for new insight and innovation.

Managed well, the combined motivation and commitment of a group of people can bring with it energy and enthusiasm. Consequently, school leaders who adopt a coaching approach when they lead senior leadership teams can unlock considerable resources that may have been latent. It could be argued that learning how to do this well has the potential to impact the school even more significantly than any one-to-one coaching conversations in which a school leader might be involved. In other words, using a coaching approach with teams, while a more complex interaction, can deliver significant benefits within school environments.

COACHING TIPS: Leveraging Multiple Voices

Although multi-voice conversations are more complex than one-to-one conversations, there are helpful ways of harnessing the various voices:

- Consider using short, focused, paired or small-group conversations within the larger team discussion.

- Make thinking "visible" as a way of contributing to more inclusive team conversations. Displaying emerging insights and points for exploration and discussion on whiteboards or other electronic or paper-based methods helps make thinking explicit and in itself helps facilitate the conversation.

- Consider use of techniques that offer opportunities for all team members to speak. This helps ensure that no one is squeezed out of the discussion by more vocal team members.

- Rotate the meeting leader role so that various team members get an opportunity to facilitate the conversations.

WHAT ARE THE DIFFERENCES BETWEEN COACHING "GROUPS" AND COACHING "TEAMS"?

Sometimes the terms *group* and *team* are used interchangeably, but there are some key differences that have relevance for the way a coaching approach can be used.

Groups typically differ from teams in the following ways:

- Groups usually come together for a specific one-off purpose.
- Groups do not expect to remain together over a long period of time.

- Groups are united by a common interest without being interdependent.

- Groups can be larger than typical work teams.

In contrast, work teams meet regularly. They expect an ongoing relationship with each other, and team members recognize that they are dependent on one another. In *The Wisdom of Teams,* Katzenbach and Smith (1993) define a team as "a small number of people with complementary skills who are committed to a common purpose, performance goals and an approach for which they hold themselves mutually accountable" (p. 111).

WHAT ARE SOME OF THE IMPORTANT ROLES TEAM LEADERS CAN PLAY WHEN USING A COACHING APPROACH WITH TEAMS?

School leaders adopt a wide range of roles in their work. At various times, they are managers, leaders, facilitators, coaches, and educators. In an exploration of complex adaptive systems, Cavanagh (2006) suggests that some of the ideas emerging from this field can be helpful for team leaders and those supporting the work of teams. The roles outlined below can be helpful to incorporate into a leader's way of working with teams.

- Systems advisor: Given that teams fulfill many of the characteristics of complex adaptive systems, it is helpful if a leader brings some awareness of systems theory to her work. For example, an understanding of the value that diversity of perspectives can bring to a team will help in team member selection and in managing any discomfort when disagreements occur.

- Mindful facilitator: When more people get involved in the conversation, it is more important for a leader to bring a high level of mindfulness into the way she facilitates the team. If mindfulness is an important capability for coaches working in one-to-one contexts, it is even more critical in a team conversation context (Brown & Grant, 2010).

- Compassionate disrupter: Disturbance of the system is one way in which it is moved from a state of equilibrium toward the "edge of chaos" where variety, tension, and creativity can lead to new possibilities. It is argued that actively disrupting existing patterns is necessary to generate new ways of thinking. Those in leadership roles will enhance their effectiveness if they are willing to be compassionately disruptive (Holman, 2010, p. 155). It is important that the role of disrupter is balanced in a way that generates an acceptable level of tension while providing support so that genuine dialogue ensues. Getting this balance right is likely to be a worthwhile but ongoing challenge.

- **Connection builder:** A high level of connectivity between team members has been identified as an important contributor to idea generation and innovation (Regine & Levine, 2000). Research by Dutton (2003) exploring "high quality connections" and studies exploring social networks (Cross & Parker, 2004) have highlighted ways in which routine interactions and communication patterns can be enhanced to deliver positive team outcomes. A good leader will nurture and stimulate connections across the team both through structural initiatives when the team is "apart" and through skilled facilitation when the team is "together."

- **Conflict optimizer:** Helping teams hold the tensions associated with uncertainty and differing perspectives is a rare and important skill to bring to effective leadership. As distinct from conflict management, the *conflict optimizer* role does not seek necessarily to resolve conflict but to help a team tease out tension, explore it, and hold the discomfort to lead to generative solutions (Edmondson, 2012; Isaacs, 1999; Kaner, et al., 1996).

Two important additional aspects need to be considered when a team leader seeks to adopt a coaching approach with her team: The difference in power between a team leader and the various team members creates a unique challenge. If a team leader has supervisory responsibility for individual team members, this can undermine the level of trust and safety between the leader and specific team members, and between the leader and the team as a whole.

Stanier (2016) has written helpfully about this, outlining factors that contribute to the perceived level of risk and safety in a relationship. When there is a real or perceived difference in power, team members are likely to ask, at least to themselves, "Will this power be used against me or us? Can I raise this topic without suffering negative consequences?"

How the power differential is made explicit and managed is a key factor in effective leadership coaching. This is made more difficult in a team context because multiple relationships are involved. Some ways in which leaders can manage this include:

- Clarifying roles within the team, including explicit reference to role of the leader

- Clarifying ground rules, particularly about how decisions will be made

- Genuinely listening

- Showing interest in the positions of others and being flexible

- Delegating decision making appropriately

COACHING TIPS: Managing Team Leader Roles

In managing these various roles while using a coaching approach it can help to:

- Be open and transparent about decision-making boundaries. That is, on what issues the team will be able to make consensus decisions and on what issues the leader might need to make a final call

- Continually and explicitly work to build trust. One way to do this is to be "loyal to the person not in the room" (Covey, 1989). That is, avoid talking about team members to others when they are not there

- Seek feedback from the team regularly and be seen to be responding to it even if this means an explanation regarding why you cannot act on a specific piece of feedback

- Seek feedback about team effectiveness from external stakeholders

- Bring a positive, constructive perspective to the expression of differences

- Develop skills to creatively, engagingly, and productively facilitate team meetings so that they conclude with a sense of progress and movement

In addition, the team leader is also a part of the team system and is therefore an integral component of what contributes to team success. This situation can lead to significant blind spot areas. A team leader can sometimes contribute to dysfunctional team performance. For example, the team leader may be unable to delegate well and so may become a "bottleneck" that hinders team task achievement; the team leader may have problematic relationships with particular team members, which impact negatively on levels of trust within the whole team. It is clearly much more difficult for a team leader to explore these unhelpful teamwork patterns in the same ways as an external coach might. Those leaders who bring a level of self-awareness and awareness of others contribute greatly toward their team's success.

When Teams Think Together: Team Thinking Framework—The Three-Legged Stool

A good way to think about how you can maximize the "intellectual capital" people bring to a meeting is through the "The Three-Legged Stool of Team Thinking." As with any three-legged stool, all three "legs" must be in place to provide stability. The three legs essential for an effective meeting are: good data, good interpersonal skills, and using a structured, visible process to maintain direction and focus and track emerging ideas.

The first leg is the need to bring good information to the meeting. Have the participants done their homework? If good information is not brought to the meeting, all the thinking done during the group's time together will be potentially flawed.

While good information is an essential starting point, it will not be used well if communication within the group is poor. The stool's second leg is, therefore, the need for good interpersonal skills. The specific skills needed include: active listening, clean and clear discussion of points of disagreement, and specific constructive expression of agreement. Active listening and the need to manage disagreement may seem self-evident. However, constructive agreement is also essential so that good ideas are developed and built on, not just agreed to without further thought.

The third leg of the stool is the need to bring a structured, visible process to the way ideas are considered and developed. This is where the GROWTH model fits well since it provides an emerging visual record of the team's thoughts as they are funneled through the GROWTH framework.

HOW CAN LEADERS USE THE 5PS FRAMEWORK FOR TEAM EFFECTIVENESS?

When working with teams, as with individuals, it can be helpful to identify relevant team effectiveness frameworks that lead to excellent performance. Such frameworks can be useful if they are deployed flexibly. Over the years, several such frameworks for team effectiveness have been proposed (e.g., Hackman, 2002; LaFasto & Larson, 2001).

In the interests of simplicity and usability, we propose the 5Ps framework for team effectiveness. Adapted from the work of Stanier (2016), the simple framework provides a way of capturing the key contributors to team effectiveness. It also highlights areas that teams need to get right if they are to achieve ongoing success:

- Purpose
- Projects
- People
- Processes
- Patterns

Purpose

Why does this team exist? It all starts at this point. Often this fundamental question is clearly established at team formation stage, but can sometimes get lost in the busyness of the team's projects and tasks. It is worth reconnecting with the team purpose regularly.

A focus on this area would see teams seeking to clarify:

- Why do we exist?
- Which key stakeholders do we serve?
- What do we need to deliver for those stakeholders?
- What do we each bring to the team for this?

Projects

This focus area highlights the importance of the work of the team, its goals, and all the tasks and work that the team undertakes to support its purpose.

A focus on this area would see teams seeking to clarify:

- How might we ensure we are clear on our priority goals?
- How might we ensure we are clear on the various tasks needing to be undertaken to achieve our goals?
- How might we measure the progress being made on these goals, tasks, and projects?

People

This focus area highlights the importance of roles, relationships, and communication.

A focus on this area would see teams seeking to clarify:

- How might we become clear on the roles we each play in this team, and how can we maintain that?
- How might we communicate with each other clearly and efficiently?
- How might we ensure that trust is strong in this team?
- Who else might need to be involved?
- How might we ensure that we collaborate in ways that draw on strengths of various team members?

Processes

This focus area highlights the importance of team procedures and ways of working, meeting, communicating, decision making, and managing differences.

A focus on this area would see teams seeking to clarify:

- How will we manage meeting time?
- How will we resolve differences?
- How will we ensure high quality thinking about challenges and opportunities?
- How will we communicate in between formal team meetings?

Patterns

This focus area highlights the importance of understanding the dynamics of the team and the various patterns of interacting that impact each of these areas.

A focus on this area would see teams seeking to clarify:

- How might we understand how team dynamics play out in constructive ways?
- How might we become aware of emerging research about team effectiveness?

In relation to this point, seminal research by Losada and Heaphy (2004) has highlighted a number of dimensions related to positive conversational quality and its impact on team performance. Their study found that several specific ways of "team talking" were correlated with higher levels of team performance:

- The ratio of "positive to negative" comments. High-performing teams had a higher ratio of positive to negative comments.
- The ratio of "inquiry to advocacy" comments. Higher-performing team members operated from a position of inquiry rather than rigidly advocating particular positions.
- The ratio of "self to other"-focused comments. Higher-performing teams were able to approach topics incorporating a wider perspective rather than a self-focused perspective that focused on how a particular topic might impact their region or their department.

An awareness and understanding of team effectiveness research can provide a basis for exploring how the team is working and help replace less helpful patterns of working with those leading to higher levels of achievement and well-being.

The GROWTH Model: A Structured, Visible Team Thinking Process

The GROWTH coaching model can be used in the following way to support high quality team thinking about a specific outcome, such as the successful implementation of a common project. It can also be a useful process to apply in resolving a relevant team challenge. The goal selected may relate to organizational requirements or it may be based on an identified need of the team. Using the GROWTH model in this way provides a visible, structured way to guide the team's thinking on a particular issue.

The first step is to agree a specific goal that is important enough for the team to commit to devoting an amount of time to progress. It needs to be related to something that the team would like to be different and which team members are prepared to do something about. Once the goal has been identified and shaped into a clear and specific statement of the preferred future, the following questions provide a way to progress thinking on the topic:

Goal

What are the benefits of us achieving this goal?

What are the costs if we don't do anything about this goal?

What will we notice about our stakeholders when we achieve this?

What will we be doing differently when we achieve this?

How will that enhance our effectiveness?

How will our results improve?

Tips

- Write comments on a whiteboard for all to see. Helping make the emerging thinking visible usually adds value to the process.
- A mixture of both small-group discussion and sharing with the wider team can be helpful during this stage.

Reality

What do we already have in place that will help us achieve this goal?

What other resources might we have that can assist us in achieving this goal?

On a scale of 1 to 10, where 10 equals our goal being achieved and 1 means no progress at all, where would you place the team currently? How come we scored this high and not lower? What else?

Options

If the team is large, consider working in smaller subgroups. Invite them to think freely about the various strategies for achieving the goal.

Ask subgroups to select a few ideas to share with the wider group.

Tips

- Keep energy levels high and move fast.
- You may wish to remind team members of some of the guidelines for idea generation:
  - Accept every idea without judgment.
  - Build on the ideas of others.
  - Move fast.
  - Do not focus on the *how* or *why* of implementing the idea.

Will

With the wider team, agree on a priority order related to the various options that might be pursued.

Tactics

Again depending on the size of the team, use small groups or the entire team to identify a few next steps and allocate responsibilities.

Tips

Make sure all actions are expressed in terms of who does what by when.

Record all next step actions so they can all be seen and the whole team can see what is being agreed to and who is involved.

Habits

Invite comment and discussion around:

- What do we need to be more of as a team to really follow through and achieve this goal?
- What will we do to keep each other accountable to the actions we have agreed on today?

Again, make visible, agree, and confirm any new actions that might emerge during this stage.

AGREEMENT GRADIENT
(ADAPTED FROM KANER ET AL., 1996)

A helpful way to facilitate group conversations in which differences of opinion are likely involves using a couple of simple practices:

1. One of these involves establishing a clear definition of consensus. Sometimes people feel that this means total unanimity. A preferred definition is "I can live with that and support it."

2. Another involves the use of the Agreement Gradient in your group thinking sessions.

   On a flip chart, draw a continuum scale with 5 points clearly marked: 1—Disagree and Cannot Support; 2—Disagree but Will Support; 3—Mixed Feelings; 4—Agree With Reservations; 5—Endorse.

   Using this scale gives permission for people to raise a divergent view and helps establish that disagreement does not mean either/or thinking. There are often varying shades of agreement and disagreement, and making this explicit through the Agreement Gradient helps the conversation stay constructive and move forward. If a minority of the team is at position 5 on a particular issue, it can be helpful to ask, "How might this course of action be modified so that you could support it?" Such a question can often lead to significant amendment or even a very different course of action emerging.

Watch It in Practice

Using a Coaching Approach With Teams

 In this chapter, we have considered the ways in which leaders can work with groups and teams of students and staff. This video further explores aspects of using a coaching approach when working with teams in an educational setting.

resources.corwin.com/campbellcoaching

CONCLUSION

A leader using a coaching approach helps teams to think together well, relate together well, and learn together well so that they can achieve more, maintain themselves in optimal working order and ensure ongoing success. A leader who uses a coaching approach often works with a team in an ongoing way. She will bring many of the skills of a team facilitator but quite a bit more to help the team function effectively—not only when it meets together but when the team is apart. In fact, school leaders who can bring a coaching approach to the way they lead their teams provide a platform for bringing out the best in one of the most significant resources within the school. Unleashing the potential of people working together in highly effective school leadership teams brings the possibility of growth and change in many areas of school life.

EXPLORE FURTHER

- To learn more about complex adaptive systems and the relevance of this concept for teams, read Holman's *Engaging Emergence*.

- To learn more about team effectiveness in general, read Lencioni's *The Five Dysfunctions of a Team*.

- To learn more about coaching organizational work teams, read Hawkins' *Leadership Team Coaching*.

- To learn more about building connections in teams, read Dutton's *Energize Your Workplace*.

SMALL STEP STARTER

Reflect for a moment on any team in which you are involved as a team member:

- Undertake a self-assessment mini snapshot across the 5Ps areas. At this point in time, how would you rate each member of this team in each of the five P areas: **Purpose; Projects; People; Processes; Patterns**? What are you noticing that supports your ratings?

- What would you be noticing in this team if each of these ratings was 1 point higher? Be as specific as you can.

- Which of these identified 5Ps areas would have the most impact on the team's effectiveness if it were to move one point higher?

- What's one action you might do in the next week, as a team member, to move toward this?

REFERENCES

Brown, S. W., & Grant, A. M. (2010). From GROW to GROUP: Theoretical issues and a practical model for group coaching in organizations. *Coaching: An International Journal of Theory, Research and Practice, 3*(1), 30–45.

Cavanagh, M. (2006). Coaching from a systemic perspective: A complex adaptive conversation. In D. R. Stober, & A. M. Grant (Eds.), *Evidence based coaching handbook* (pp. 313–354) Hoboken, NJ: Wiley & Sons.

Covey, S. R. (1989). *The 7 habits of highly effective people: Restoring the character ethic.* New York, NY: Fireside.

Cross, R., & Parker, A. (2004). *The hidden power of social networks: How work really gets done in organizations.* Boston, MA: HBR Press.

Dutton, J. E. (2003). *Energize your workplace: How to create and sustain high-quality connections at work.* San Francisco, CA: Jossey-Bass.

Edmondson, A. (2012). *Teaming: How organizations learn, innovate, and compete in the knowledge economy.* San Francisco, CA: Jossey-Bass.

Hackman, R. J. (2002). *Leading teams: Setting the stage for great performances.* Boston, MA: Harvard Business School Press.

Hawkins, P. (2011). *Leadership team coaching: Developing collective transformational leadership.* London, UK: Kogan Page.

Holman, P. (2010). *Engaging emergence: Turning upheaval into opportunity.* San Francisco, CA: Berrett-Koehler.

Isaacs, W. (1999). *Dialogue and the art of thinking together. A pioneering approach to communicating in business and in life.* New York, NY: Double Day.

Kaner, S., Lind, L., Toldi, C., Fisk, S., & Berger, D. (1996). *Facilitator's guide to participatory decision-making.* Gabriola Is., BC: New Society.

Katzenbach, J. R., & Smith, D. K. (1993). *The wisdom of teams: Creating the high-performance organization.* New York, NY: Collins Business Essentials.

LaFasto, F. M. J., & Larson, C. E. (2001). *When teams work best: 6,000 team members and leaders tell what it takes to succeed.* Thousand Oaks, CA: SAGE.

Lencioni, P. (2002). *The five dysfunctions of a team: A leadership fable.* San Francisco, CA: Jossey-Bass.

Losada, M., & Heaphy, E. (2004). The role of positivity and connectivity in the performance of business teams: A nonlinear dynamic model. *American Behavioral Scientist, 47*(6), 740.

Stanier, M. B. (2016). *The coaching habit: Say less, ask more, and change the way you lead forever.* Toronto, Ontario, Canada: Box of Crayons Press.

Regine, B., & Lewin, R. (2000). Leading at the edge: How leaders influence complex systems. *Emergence, 2*(2), 5–23.

CHAPTER 9

Leading a Coaching Culture

The question of coaching cultures in educational settings is one that will be of interest to all school leaders. We believe that this concept could have a positive and meaningful impact on learners, educators, and leadership teams. And yet, while the question is of particular interest, the answer is less straightforward. In this chapter, we explore the question further, recognizing from the outset that there may be no easy answers.

As with most conversations related to coaching, it is helpful to start with definitions. Once we have moved closer to a shared definition of *coaching cultures*, we consider the evidence that supports the use of coaching in organizational settings. This is followed by a survey of some ideas about how coaching cultures might be developed. The chapter concludes with practical ways for educators to foster such cultures in their institutions.

DEFINING OUR TERMS

We have already defined *coaching* in relation to its use in education contexts. But what of *culture*? Even though we use the word so often in everyday interactions that it seems to be a familiar concept, it is relatively difficult to define. According to Edgar Schein (2010), culture is a "pattern of shared, basic taken-for-granted assumptions . . . that manifests itself at the level of observable artifacts and shared espoused values, norms, and rules of behavior" (p. 32). When considering cultures in educational settings, Nuri-Robins, Lindsey, Lindsey, and Terrell (2006) have defined culture simply as the beliefs and practices shared by a group. While accepting that the concept of culture is intensely complex, we define it in straightforward terms (for the purposes of this chapter) as the *taken-for-granted* assumptions, beliefs, and practices of a group. In the context of this book, this means that we focus on the assumptions, beliefs, and practices that are most conducive to positive learning environments.

THE CURRENT STATE OF PLAY

In this section, we share current thinking about coaching cultures and then survey the proposed benefits of using coaching within professional contexts. A recent review of the academic literature about coaching cultures (Gormley & van Nieuwerburgh, 2014) identified broad agreement of the following:

"Coaching can form an integral part of how organizations develop their people."

By considering case studies of successful implementation of coaching initiatives, it becomes apparent that the use of coaching with professionals is a positive way of supporting their growth and development. There are two ways in which coaching is used in this context. First, professionals are offered coaching about how to enhance performance within their current job roles. Second, coaching can be very effective in supporting the implementation of learning from training or professional development activities.

"Coaching can be embedded within regular performance management processes."

While the survey of the literature has suggested that this is becoming more prevalent, we have some questions about this way of using coaching. In theory, the use of coaching can be used to transform performance management conversations from relatively operational conversations about the achievement of professional targets to more dynamic conversations about learning and development. While this is a laudable aim, we have already shared our concern that the integration of performance management and coaching can cause confusion about professional roles and boundaries. We believe that coaching is a nonjudgmental, nonevaluative conversation. When integrated into an organizational process in which it could be argued that it is the *role* of the performance manager to judge and evaluate the performance of an individual, we believe that the risks of mixed messages and confusion are great. Questions can also be raised about the ability of the reviewee to be fully open and honest during the coaching part of the conversation. We have argued in this book that it is more useful to think of leaders using a coaching approach when conducting performance review conversations. This would align more comfortably with the principles of coaching and good leadership. The use of a coaching approach is explored in more detail in Chapter 6.

"Coaching can demonstrate a commitment to support the professional growth of individuals within an organization."

This is frequently reported within the academic literature and by organizations that have implemented coaching initiatives within professional contexts.

The provision of coaching is widely understood as an explicit demonstration of an organization's commitment to the growth and development of its people. Therefore, simply providing staff with access to coaching (should they want it) can have a positive impact within educational settings. Anecdotally, many of our own coachees in educational settings recognize this, too. The fact that the school, college, or university has invested in providing them with an opportunity to receive coaching is often appreciated and taken as a sign of support and encouragement. However, we believe that it is important to reflect on how this is managed. There are many examples of organizations that do provide coaching across a large number of staff, but sometimes this is limited to senior and middle managers. We would argue that this might have some positive impact on those who have access to coaching but is likely to have a larger negative effect across the organization if it is felt that some people are excluded. In other words, access to coaching is seen as evidence of the organization valuing staff—so those who do not have access inevitably feel less valued or appreciated.

"Creating a coaching culture requires investment and can take time."

This may be unwelcome news for some, but it is an important point that bears emphasizing. The case studies and academic articles are consistent in showing that coaching cultures require investment of time and resources. In many cases, such cultures have developed over many years. By their very nature, cultures are very complex and take time to develop. The resources required are discussed later in this chapter.

"Creating a coaching culture can lead to changes in the organization with rewards for staff, stakeholders, and clients."

Although it should be recognized that time and resources are needed, the academic literature shows that working toward a coaching culture can lead to changes within an organization that are experienced positively by everyone concerned. In educational settings, this could mean positive outcomes for learners, educators, parents, and members of the educational community.

Based on this review of what is known about coaching cultures, Gormley and van Nieuwerburgh (2014) propose the following definition: "[C]oaching cultures exist when a group of people embrace coaching as a way of making holistic improvements to individuals *and* the organization through formal and informal coaching interactions. This can mean a large proportion of individuals adopting coaching behaviours to relate to, support, and influence one another and their stakeholders" (p. 92). As we have discussed in this chapter, the initial experiences and academic study of such cultures indicate that it can generate benefits for everyone involved. In the section below, we consider these benefits.

PROPOSED BENEFITS

Coaching initiatives are reported to generate a number of positive outcomes when used in professional contexts (van Nieuwerburgh, 2016). In a meta-analysis of all quantitative studies undertaken until 2016, it has been suggested that coaching interventions can have significant positive effects on performance, skills, well-being, coping, goal attainment, and attitudes to work (Theeboom, 2016). More specifically, a number of studies and professional evaluations of coaching initiatives in organizational settings showed positive effects on a number of key areas that are of interest to educators and senior leadership teams.

The Benefits of Coaching

Increases in self-awareness and emotional intelligence (EQ)	Carter, Fairhurst, Markwick, & Miller, 2009
Improved interpersonal skills leading to better relationships	Carter et al., 2009; McKee, Tilin, & Mason, 2009
Increased self-confidence	Carter et al., 2009
Improved leadership skills	Carter et al., 2009; McKee et al., 2009; Mukherjee, 2012
Better work-life balance	Carter et al., 2009
Increased loyalty to the organization	McKee et al., 2009
Renewed passion to support the development of others	McKee et al., 2009

SOURCE: Adapted from van Nieuwerburgh, C. (Ed.). (2016). *Coaching in professional contexts.* London, UK: SAGE.

HOW TO WORK TOWARD A COACHING CULTURE

If we accept the proposed benefits cited above, then the creation, development, and ongoing support for coaching cultures could reasonably become a priority for educational leaders. A number of texts have proposed a staged process for the creation of such cultures. These are based on practical experience and have been formulated by retrospectively considering the steps taken by organizations with positive coaching cultures. The great strength of such an approach is that it is rooted in practice. Therefore, the proposed stages are pragmatic and implementable. The most often-cited process for developing coaching cultures is that developed by Hawkins (2012). An overview of the seven-step model is presented below.

The Seven Steps Toward a Coaching Culture

1. Recruiting external coaches and/or consultants

2. Creating internal coaching capacity

3. Ensuring leadership support for coaching

4. Enabling organizational learning from coaching initiatives

5. Including coaching within performance management processes

6. Adopting a coaching style of leadership

7. Using a coaching approach as a way of doing business

SOURCE: Adapted from Hawkins, P. (2012). *Creating a coaching culture.* Maidenhead, Berkshire, UK: Open University Press.

According to Hawkins (2012), the process should be initiated by procuring external coaches to provide coaching to senior executives. These coaches can then be used to train internal staff in coaching-related skills. As this is developing, it is important that the leadership of the organization explicitly and actively support the implementation of coaching initiatives. Hawkins underlines the importance of ensuring organizational learning through these initiatives. He proposes that coaching should be embedded within performance management processes. Through these initiatives, coaching could be promoted as the preferred way of managing within the organization. Finally, once coaching is embedded within the organization, it can be used to interact with clients and stakeholders.

A potential drawback of using case studies of successful organizations to retrospectively identify steps toward a coaching culture is the assumption that the process would apply in other professional contexts. Indeed, every school's situation is bound to be different, and leaders will be best placed to make decisions about the steps needed to move toward a coaching culture. However, we also believe that the key principles may be transferable across organizations.

COACHING CULTURES IN EDUCATIONAL CONTEXTS

In an earlier attempt to understand the concept of coaching cultures in educational contexts, van Nieuwerburgh and Passmore (2012) had proposed the idea of "coaching cultures for learning," arguing that "successful implementation of coaching cultures within school (based on proven coaching principles) can lead to improved environments for learning. This, in turn, will mean better results for students, staff, and the wider community" (p. 153). According to this approach, the concept of a coaching culture for learning was based on the idea of transferring what is powerful about one-to-one coaching conversations into the everyday culture of schools. While it is proposed that those leading the move toward a coaching culture would select the elements of effective coaching practice they would like to see demonstrated in the school culture, a few characteristics were cited as examples: mutual trust (between coach and coachee), timeliness (of the intervention), awareness of the need for change (on the part of the coachee), ownership of goals (on the part of the coachee), supportive relationships (between coach and coachee), genuine care (on the part of the coach) and a positive outlook (as the nature of the interaction) (p. 155).

Van Nieuwerburgh and Passmore (2012) suggest using the Appreciative Inquiry (AI) process (Srivastra, Fry, & Cooperrider, 1990) to engage stakeholders and work toward a coaching culture. The four-step AI process comprises the following stages: Discovery; Dream; Design; and Destiny. Readers who wish to use this approach may find it helpful to read more about the AI process. There are many good sources of information online. *The Appreciative Inquiry Handbook: For Leaders of Change* is a key textbook for practitioners. When using AI in an educational setting, the school community might work collectively and collaboratively through the four stages, responding to the following questions that align with AI process:

Discovery:

- "What's working well at the moment?"
- "What is our signature strength?"

Dream:

- "What can we achieve together that would make us proud?"

Design:

- "What will a coaching culture look and feel like?"

Destiny:

- "How will we feel when we have achieved a coaching culture?"
- "What is already in place?"
- "What else needs to happen?"

We must avoid temptations to suggest that this is a framework that will work for all educational institutions. Evidently, there will be many ways of implementing this process. The important driver for this approach is the attempt to involve as many people as possible, enabling them collectively to imagine an exciting future and celebrate existing strengths. The energy generated from such an approach could provide the impetus for making adaptations to current practices to move closer to the vision of a coaching culture.

GLOBAL FRAMEWORK

Another approach is to allow such a culture to develop organically. As we continue to investigate the concept of coaching cultures in educational settings, we believe that coaching cultures can emerge as educational institutions intentionally (and in good faith) implement coaching initiatives for the benefit of learners, educators, and the community. In this regard, the Global Framework for Coaching in Education (van Nieuwerburgh & Campbell, 2015) can be helpful when making decisions about appropriate interventions. Coaching is a conversational process that can be used to achieve *something*. Introducing coaching into an educational setting should not be an end in itself, but a way of achieving meaningful outcomes for the coachees and the institution.

EDUCATIONAL LEADERSHIP

Supporting, encouraging, and developing excellent leadership practice is certainly one part of working toward a coaching culture. As we have seen above, the engagement of an organization's leaders is a critical first step. Any initiatives that will demonstrate the full engagement and support of the leadership of an organization are likely to support the development of coaching cultures.

Some examples:

- Educational leaders explicitly endorse the use of coaching.
- Educational leaders create time and space for coaching to take place.
- Educational leaders regularly receive coaching.
- Educational leaders make coaching available to all school staff.
- Educational leaders ensure that coaching initiatives are built into their institutions' strategic plans.

PROFESSIONAL PRACTICE

In educational settings, there is a natural and welcome focus on learning and development. Coaching initiatives that encourage the improvement of the professional practice of all staff in educational settings would seem to be central to a coaching culture. Of equal importance is the availability of coaching to support the well-being of staff in schools, colleges, and universities. We recognize that the well-being of educators is essential in itself, but we would argue that having well-supported, physically and mentally healthy educators will increase the likelihood of positive, supportive learning organizations.

Some examples:

- Staff in schools are open to feedback and coaching to improve their professional practice.
- Staff have the right to request a trained coach whenever they want such support.
- Staff are trained in coaching skills so that they can provide support to one another.
- Staff are able to use a coaching approach with colleagues, educational leaders, and learners and their parents or caregivers.

COMMUNITY

It has been recognized that improved connections between educational institutions and their communities can reap rewards for students (Sanders, 2006). A coaching culture would reach out to its community and wider group of stakeholders. As Hawkins (2012) has argued, once an organization has implemented a coaching culture, it becomes possible for the institution to communicate with its stakeholders using a coaching approach. In practice, this could mean open and two-way dialogue with parents and caregivers; an inclusive approach that welcomes parents and caregivers into schools to continue learning and also to support enrichment activities.

Some examples:

- Parents and caregivers are offered training in coaching-related skills to support the learning of their children.
- Parents and caregivers volunteer to coach or mentor staff or students in the school.
- Educators use a coaching approach during parent/teacher conferences.
- Involving parents and caregivers in discussions about developing coaching cultures.

STUDENT SUCCESS AND WELL-BEING

Ultimately, coaching cultures should enhance the learning environment for students so that they can achieve more of their potential while also enhancing their well-being. A coaching culture would support this by creating an environment in which all members of the community would feel valued and supported.

Some examples:

- Training students to become coaches so that they can support other students.

- Students using a coaching approach when engaging in community projects to solve social and environmental problems.

- Educators and students learning about coaching together.

POINTS FOR CONSIDERATION

Due to the complexity and variety of organizational settings, and the similar complexity and variety of human beings, it is difficult to imagine that there will ever be a blueprint of how to create a coaching culture. Every institution is different; every person is different; therefore, every situation is different when it comes to fostering a coaching culture. While we have surveyed a number of possible ways in which coaching initiatives can be introduced into organizational settings, we remain committed to the idea that groups of educators should take responsibility for developing such cultures within their institutions. Below are some key points that may increase the likelihood of success.

- It is up to a group of educators to decide whether and how to introduce the idea of a coaching culture in their institution. The impetus and drive for such a culture must come from within.

- People within the organization should identify where coaching interventions will have the biggest impact. The Global Framework for Coaching in Education provides possible areas of focus.

- The leaders of an organization should be fully supportive of the idea and demonstrate their commitment in practice.

- When an area of focus is selected, any coaching initiatives should be introduced tentatively, adhering to the principle of "democratic voluntary involvement" (van Nieuwerburgh, 2016). In other words, no one should be excluded from the opportunity of benefiting from the coaching initiatives; every person should have choice about whether she wishes to get involved; and if a person chooses to get involved, there should be meaningful ways to do so.

- It is helpful to be clear about the desired outcome of such coaching initiatives. Being explicit about success criteria will enable everyone to see the benefits of coaching and will allow for evaluation.

AWKWARD QUESTIONS

It would be nice to end the chapter with the points above. However, there is still more to learn about coaching cultures, so we pose some unanswered questions below.

Can we ever achieve a coaching culture?

It may be the case that some of the characteristics of a coaching culture may make it difficult to ever declare that an organization has "achieved" a coaching culture. Almost by definition, the culture is continually evolving and responsive to the needs of its people. A coaching culture should probably always be open to new ideas and developments.

Should organizations set out to develop a coaching culture?

It could be argued that the development of coaching cultures is a by-product of people working together to achieve important and meaningful objectives. That is why we suggest that coaching initiatives should be focused on areas of need within educational settings, using the Global Framework for Coaching in Education. By starting to use a range of coaching initiatives to improve outcomes for learners and educators, a coaching culture may develop organically.

How can coaching cultures be evaluated?

It is difficult to single out key indicators of a coaching culture. As suggested above, the existence of a coaching culture may facilitate the achievement of important goals and objectives. In other words, a coaching culture can make it easier for an educational institution to achieve important goals by enhancing the well-being and improving the performance of educators and learners. Perhaps one way of checking if such a culture exists is to ask people in the organization.

Are there any pre-conditions before an organization can start to develop a coaching culture?

This question is often asked. It originates from the belief that some organizations are not ready to embark on the journey toward a coaching culture. Certainly, there are organizations that do not consider working toward a coaching culture to be a priority. If there are other pressing and urgent initiatives, people in an organization may rightly decide to prioritize those. Some of the preconditions posited (good communication, culture of openness, high level of trust) are also the reasons that organizations wish to introduce a coaching culture.

Are we simply talking about a positive learning culture?

If the outcome of a coaching culture is an organization in which people feel supported, valued, and encouraged to flourish, then isn't this just a positive learning culture? We are not sure about the answer to this at the moment. As long as the end result is a learning environment that allows people to grow and develop in a way that unlocks their potential while enhancing their well-being, perhaps it doesn't matter what we call it.

Watch It in Practice

Additional Perspectives on a Coaching Culture

In this chapter, we have addressed the interesting concept of "coaching cultures." This video shares further insights about establishing a coaching culture.

resources.corwin.com/campbellcoaching

CONCLUSION

This chapter has considered the currently popular notion of *coaching cultures*. Starting with a discussion of key terms, we have surveyed the existing academic literature, drawing a few conclusions based on ideas that consistently emerge from research and practice. Some ideas for working toward coaching cultures are presented, although we conclude on a cautionary note. There is still much to learn about the idea of "a coaching culture." The good news is that there seems to be a perfect fit between the purpose and intention of schools and the potential benefits of coaching cultures. So we encourage educational institutions to focus on creating learning environments that create the conditions for the well-being and success of learners, educators and all the key stakeholders.

EXPLORE FURTHER

- To learn more about coaching cultures in general, read Gormley and van Nieuwerburgh's "Developing Coaching Cultures: A Review of the Literature."

- To learn more about coaching cultures in schools, read van Nieuwerburgh and Passmore's "Creating Coaching Cultures for Learning."

- To learn more about coaching cultures in non-school environments, read Hawkins' *Creating a Coaching Culture*.

SMALL STEP STARTER

Take a few moments to think about how you might describe the culture in your school. Jot down in bullet points the key factors of your school's culture.

Now take the view of the following stakeholders. Next to each bullet point, make a note of how each would experience the key factors you listed:

- A student

- An educator

- A governor

- A parent

- A member of the school community

One way to tell that you have a strong culture is that all your stakeholders can predict fairly accurately how the school will respond to various situations.

REFERENCES

Carter, A., Fairhurst, P., Markwick, C., & Miller, L. (2009). *Evaluation of West Midlands coaching pool.* IES Paper, West Midlands Regional Improvement and Efficiency Partnership.

Gormley, H., & van Nieuwerburgh, C. (2014). Developing coaching cultures: A review of the literature. *Coaching: An International Journal of Theory, Research and Practice, 7*(1), 90–101.

Hawkins, P. (2012). *Creating a coaching culture.* Maidenhead, Berkshire, UK: Open University Press.

McKee, A., Tilin, F., & Mason, D. (2009). Coaching from the inside: Building an internal group of emotionally intelligent coaches. *International Coaching Psychology Review, 4*(1), 59–70.

Mukherjee, S. (2012). Does coaching transform coaches? A case study in internal coaching. *International Journal of Evidence Based Coaching and Mentoring, 10*(2), 76–87.

Nuri-Robins, K., Lindsey, R. B, Lindsey, D. B., & Terrell, R. D. (2006). *Culturally proficient instruction: A guide for people who teach* (2nd ed.). Thousand Oaks, CA: Corwin.

Sanders, M. (2006). *Building school-community partnerships: Collaboration for student success.* Thousand Oaks, CA: Corwin.

Schein, E. (2010). *Organizational culture and leadership* (4th ed.). San Francisco, CA: Jossey-Bass.

Srivastra, S., Fry, R. E., & Cooperrider, D. L. (Eds.). (1990). *Appreciative management and leadership: The power of positive thought and action in organizations.* San Francisco, CA: Jossey-Bass.

Theeboom, T. (2016). The current state of research. In C. van Nieuwerburgh (Ed.), *Coaching in professional contexts* (pp. 187–197). London, UK: SAGE.

van Nieuwerburgh, C. (Ed.). (2016). *Coaching in professional contexts.* London, UK: SAGE.

van Nieuwerburgh, C., & Campbell, J. (2015). A global framework for coaching in education, *CoachEd: The Teaching Leaders Coaching Journal, 1,* 2–5.

van Nieuwerburgh, C., & Passmore, J. (2012). Creating coaching cultures for learning. In C. van Nieuwerburgh (Ed.), *Coaching in education: Getting better results for students, educators and parents.* London, UK: Karnac.

Visit **www.growthcoaching.com.au** for more coaching and professional learning resources for educators.

CHAPTER 10

Conclusion

We hope that you have found this book to be both thought provoking and practically useful. In the concluding chapter, we invite you to reflect on your own learning and on the complexity of leadership in current times. We wrap things up by asking you to reflect on what is most important for you. As a leader who is continually learning and developing, you are being a role model within your professional context. It is certainly important that educational leaders recognize that their actions and attitudes can influence people within the organization and its culture. At this point, it may be helpful to consider the questions in the box below:

Your Learning

- What have you learned about *coaching in education* from reading this book?

- What have you learned about yourself as you read through this book?

- How might this learning inform your leadership practice?

- What might be different for educators in your school as a result of coaching initiatives that have been introduced?

- What might be different for learners in your school as a result of coaching initiatives that have been introduced?

It is our view, outlined throughout the book, that leaders who are able to use a coaching approach are better able to navigate the challenges of leading human intensive educational institutions in the current climate. While there may still be situations in which traditional problem solving will be the best course of action, we contend that these are going to be infrequent. More often, the challenges will be complex, and encouraging educators and students to discover their own ways forward will be more effective both in the short and long term. Although there will be times when a leader will have to direct people what to do, in the majority of cases, engaging and enthusing colleagues and students will be more productive and more likely to engender engagement and well-being. Indeed we would propose that the coaching skills and approaches outlined in this book are integral to the new ways of leading that our complex organizations, schools in particular, require.

In this book, we have presented a case for adopting a coaching approach when leading in educational settings. In the first chapter, we surveyed the context of leadership in educational settings. Then, we defined the term *leadership coaching*, exploring the complexities of coaching when there is a perceived difference in power and status. In Chapters 3 and 4, we outlined the GROWTH coaching system and its conversational framework. We believe that these are valuable tools and processes for educational leaders. Then, in Chapter 5, we surveyed a number of positive, strength-based approaches and techniques that support coaching conversations. In Chapter 6, we focused on the emerging concept of a *coaching approach*. Chapter 7 addressed the related skills of giving and receiving feedback. We proposed that these are important skills for coaches that were even more critical for school leaders. In Chapter 8, we went beyond one-to-one coaching conversations to consider the implications of using a coaching approach with groups and teams. Finally, in Chapter 9, we reflected on the important role of leaders in developing coaching cultures across their educational settings.

Evidently, the role of a leader is complex and rewarding at the same time. What leaders say and do have a significant impact on the success and well-being of both educators and students. It follows, therefore, that the well-being and success of educational leaders is also important. For leaders to have the time, capacity, and energy to foster coaching cultures, it becomes essential for them to look after their own health and well-being.

Please reflect on the questions below:

Your Success and Well-Being

- Where do you get your support from?
- To what extent are you a role model for a healthy work-life balance?
- What do you do to look after your physical health?
- How do you manage your mental health?
- Who is your coach?
- How often do you reflect on and celebrate your successes?

It must be recognized that educational leadership today is challenging and that new ways of leading schools are needed (Linsky & Lawrence, 2011). At the same time, it is possible to view the role of principal as the "best job in the world" (Goddard, 2014). It is hoped that adopting a coaching approach will allow leaders to align their personal and professional values and principles. Providing the environments in which students can flourish and educators feel valued can impact the success and well-being of everyone involved. It can empower everyone in your school community, giving people more opportunity, greater confidence, and higher aspirations.

REFERENCES

Goddard, V. (2014). *Best job in the world*. Carmarthen, UK: Crown.

Linsky, M., & Lawrence, J. (2011). Adaptive challenges for school leadership. In H. O'Sullivan and J. West-Burnham (Eds.), *Leading and managing schools*. London, UK: SAGE.

Visit **www.growthcoaching.com.au** for more coaching and professional learning resources for educators.

Index

A SAGE Publishing Company

Helping educators make the greatest impact

CORWIN HAS ONE MISSION: to enhance education through intentional professional learning.

We build long-term relationships with our authors, educators, clients, and associations who partner with us to develop and continuously improve the best evidence-based practices that establish and support lifelong learning.

THE PROFESSIONAL LEARNING ASSOCIATION

Learning Forward is a nonprofit, international membership association of learning educators committed to one vision in K–12 education: Excellent teaching and learning every day. To realize that vision, Learning Forward pursues its mission to build the capacity of leaders to establish and sustain highly effective professional learning. Information about membership, services, and products is available from www.learningforward.org.

Solutions you want. Experts you trust. Results you need.

AUTHOR CONSULTING

Author Consulting

On-site professional learning with sustainable results! Let us help you design a professional learning plan to meet the unique needs of your school or district. www.corwin.com/pd

INSTITUTES

Institutes

Corwin Institutes provide collaborative learning experiences that equip your team with tools and action plans ready for immediate implementation. www.corwin.com/institutes

ECOURSES

eCourses

Practical, flexible online professional learning designed to let you go at your own pace. www.corwin.com/ecourses

READ2EARN

Read2Earn

Did you know you can earn graduate credit for reading this book? Find out how: www.corwin.com/read2earn

Contact an account manager at (800) 831-6640 or visit **www.corwin.com** for more information.